OR

D1108276

Purchased from
Multnomah County Library
Title Wave Used Bookstore
216 NE Knott St, Portland, OR
503-988-5021

NIGHT OVER TAOS

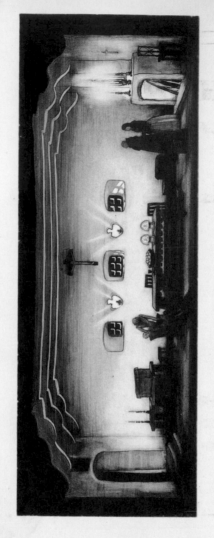

Setting for *Night over Taos* by Robert Edmond Jones, 1932

NIGHT OVER TAOS

A Play in Three Acts

BY

MAXWELL ANDERSON

SAMUEL FRENCH

New York   Los Angeles

SAMUEL FRENCH LTD. London

1932

LIBRARY ASSOCIATION
... OF ...
PORTLAND ORE.

ALL RIGHTS RESERVED

Copyright 1932, by Maxwell Anderson

CAUTION: Professionals and amateurs are hereby warned that "NIGHT OVER TAOS," being fully protected under the copyright laws of the United States of America, the British Empire, including the Dominion of Canada, and all other countries of the Copyright Union, is subject to a royalty. All rights, including professional, amateur, motion pictures, recitation, public reading, radio broadcasting, and the rights of translation into foreign languages are strictly reserved. In its present form the play is dedicated to the reading public only. All inquiries, regarding this play should be addressed to Samuel French, at 25 West 45th Street, New York, N. Y., or 811 West 7th Street, Los Angeles, Calif.

812
A54n
c4

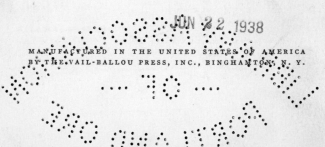

JUN 22 1938

MANUFACTURED IN THE UNITED STATES OF AMERICA
BY THE VAIL-BALLOU PRESS, INC., BINGHAMTON, N. Y.

Night Over Taos was presented by the GROUP THEATRE, INC., at the 48th Street Theatre, New York, on the night of March 9, 1932, with the following cast:

INDIAN SLAVE..................Played by		*Robert Lewis*
DONA VERA..................... "	"	*Mary Morris*
VALERIA .... "	"	*Virginia Farmer*
MARIA .... "	"	*Paula Miller*
RAQUEL .... "	"	*Margaret Barker*
CONCHITA .... "	"	*Gertrude Maynard*
NUNA .... "	"	*Phoebe Brand*
LITA .... "	"	*Eunice Stoddard*
CARLOTA .... "	"	*Dorothy Patten*
CRISTINA .... "	"	*Sylvia Feningston*
GRASO .... "	"	*Friendly Ford*
DONA JOSEFA................... "	"	*Stella Adler*
FATHER MARTINEZ.............. "	"	*Morris Carnovsky*
DIANA .... "	"	*Ruth Nelson*
DIEGO .... "	"	*Harry Bellaver*
FEDERICO .... "	"	*Franchot Tone*
NARCISO .... "	"	*Herbert Ratner*
CAPTAIN .... "	"	*Art Smith*
DON HERMANO.................. "	"	*Lewis Leverett*
DON MIGUEL................... "	"	*Sanford Meisner*
FELIPE .... "	"	*Walter Coy*
SANTOS .... "	"	*Gerrit Kraber*
PABLO MONTOYA............... "	"	*J. Edward Bromberg*
ANDRES .... "	"	*Clement Wilenchick*
DON FERNANDO................. "	"	*Luther Adler*
DON MARIO.................... "	"	*Philip Robinson*
MATEO .... "	"	*Clifford Odets*
1ST TRAPPER.................. "	"	*William Challee*
2ND TRAPPER.................. "	"	*Grover Burgess*
PEONS .... "	"	*Sylvia Hoffman*
		Byron McGrath
		Burgess Meredith
		Robert Porter

Production directed by Lee Strasberg.

DEC 12 1932

The play is laid in Taos, New Mexico, in 1847.

Act I

The great hall of the Montoya hacienda. Night.

Act II

The same. An hour later.

Act III

The same. A few minutes later.

ACT ONE

SCENE: *The great hall in the residence of* PABLO MON-
TOYA *at Taos, New Mexico, in the year 1847.*

*The room is long and low, its adobe walls white-
washed to the beamed ceiling and covered with red
tapestries to a height of four or five feet. A long table,
homemade, as is all the furniture, occupies the center,
flanked with benches and chairs. There is a large fireplace at the right and an entrance to the inner rooms
behind it. At the left a gigantic entrance door with
small altars on either side. Candles burn before both.
At the rear are three small and low windows, sunk deep
in the four-foot wall and not glazed, but covered with
translucent parchment. A large hourglass sits on a
stand near the fireplace. It is evening and dark save for
candle light.*

*A number of women and young girls, two or three of
whom have been setting the table, are weeping quietly
while they exchange news in awed voices. Those who
were supposed to be carrying in dishes have set down
their trays. An Indian* SLAVE *has been cleaning ashes
from the fireplace into a wooden bowl.* DONNA VERI,
*an old woman, has turned from giving him directions to
listen to the women.*

MARIA

And Estevan, too, is dead?

NUNA

I don't know. He didn't say.

MARIA

Yes, dead. I knew it.

LITA

Yes, dead. I knew it.

RAQUEL

Who told you this?

NUNA

Santos. Graso heard him.

CARLOTTA

But is Taos defeated?

CRISTINA

Defeated? How could Taos be defeated?

LITA

Yes. How could it be?

NUNA

He didn't say that
[GRASO, *an old peon, enters.*]

GRASO

Someone must speak to Donna Josefa . . .

MARIA

Graso! What was this news?

CRISTINA

Graso . . .
[*The Indian goes out with the ashes.*]

GRASO

Someone must speak to Donna Josefa at once. Santos, the coward, brings word and runs away! He will not come in! No, he must leave it to me!

RAQUEL

But what has happened?
[*A wailing song is heard from without.*]

GRASO

Mind you, it comes from Santos, not from me. Santos said there was a great battle, and General Montoya taken prisoner, and a great trampling and running in the snow . . . for, you see, it snowed there in the pass where they were . . .

CRISTINA

General Montoya taken! . . .

GRASO

It's not my news . . . it's Santos brings it . . . and you must tell Donna Josefa. . . . Run in and tell her, Maria.

MARIA

No, no, not I.

RAQUEL

Conchita will go. Run in, Conchita, and tell her.

CONCHITA

But what shall I tell her?

CRISTINA

That there's been a battle, and Graso is here. . . .

GRASO

No . . . say nothing about me.
[CONCHITA *goes out.*]

RAQUEL

Graso . . . what more did he say?

GRASO

No more. . . .

RAQUEL

Yes yes . . . there was something about Pedros!

GRASO

Who would believe a great liar like that when he says
General Montoya is taken prisoner by gringoes . . .
and if we cannot believe him in regard to the one thing
is it likely he spoke truth in respect to the other?

RAQUEL

Graso, for the love of our mother, is my Pedros killed?

GRASO

Pedros?

RAQUEL

Yes, Pedros! For God's love, say!

GRASO

What you have heard.

RAQUEL

He's dead!

GRASO

If one wishes to believe a great liar.

MARIA

And Estevan?

GRASO

Why, as to Estevan, no . . . I heard nothing. [*He
turns.*]

CRISTINA

Graso, look at me . . . speak not what we wish, but what is true.

LITA

Is it Americans we fight with, Maria?

MARIA

Be quiet! Yes, Americans.

GRASO

You must repeat the message to Donna Josefa . . . and tell her it is lies . . . only she must hear it. . . . [*He goes to the door.*]

VERI

Stay and tell her yourself!

GRASO

I . . . I bring no news!
[CONCHITA *returns.*]

CONCHITA

Donna Josefa wishes to see Graso!

CRISTINA

Graso . . .

GRASO

Have I prophecy? . . . I know no more! Tell her I
had gone! [*He goes out.*]

CRISTINA

Nunita!

NUNA

I don't know, Cristina.

CRISTINA

No one will tell me, I see. I must find him myself.

CARLOTTA

Where is Santos?

NUNA

He went on down to the village.

RAQUEL

But if Montoya's prisoner, then they're all taken prisoner, or dead!

CARLOTTA

We'll go after him.

CRISTINA

Yes.
[*They go toward the door.*]

VERI

How they weep, the little fat-brains! How they drip! Tender hearts, broken hearts!

CONCHITA

And why not, then? Is it any time for laughing?

VERI

Don't spit at me, little brimstone image. I know them and their race. They've no sooner one man killed over them than they've crawled under another, and more likely than not an Americano! More than once I've wondered whether the pure blood of Spain is more likely to turn dark with Indian or white with the northerners.

CRISTINA

We haven't all traveled your path, Veri.

LITA

You hear that, Veri? You hear?

VERI

You've been more places than the stations of the cross, little lambs of God!

CARLOTTA

Let her talk. [*She starts to go.*]

VERI

Only take care Mateo doesn't come home at the wrong
moment, Carlotta.

CARLOTTA

What do you mean?

VERI

Nothing.

CARLOTTA

If you mean . . .

VERI

I do mean! And why not? Let the conquerors conquer!
Only I've never had a gringo under my skirts, chiquita.

NUNA

Come, mother, let her alone.

CARLOTTA

But she lies!

VERI

Was there not one tall hunter from the north who escaped when they killed the governor?

CRISTINA

Come, Carlotta, nobody believes her.

CARLOTTA

It's all lies, lies, lies . . .

VERI

I won't say a word, I promise you.

NUNA

[*Aghast*] She's . . . she's wicked. She's as wicked as she is dirty.

VERI

All I say is you've been more places than the stations of the cross . . . [DONNA JOSEFA *enters.*] . . . and little brimstone here is the fruit of one of your trips! And Nuna is another!

JOSEFA

What is all this noise? Why are you in the hall at this hour?

RAQUEL

Forgive us, Donna Josefa. We followed Nunita in because she brought news of the battle.

JOSEFA

What news?
[*There is silence.*]
What news? Nuna?

NUNA

It was Graso that brought it, Donna Josefa.

JOSEFA

Yes . . . but . . . what was it? And where is Graso?

NUNA

It seems they both ran, Donna Josefa, both sides. And it was fought in darkness and there was snow falling on the mountain, so that nothing is sure.

JOSEFA

Is that all? Come . . . what else?
[*Another pause.*]

RAQUEL

It is said that a number of the men of Taos have been killed, Donna Josefa, and a number taken prisoner, among them General Montoya himself . . . but we know this to be untrue.

JOSEFA

How do you know it to be untrue?

RAQUEL

We cannot believe that, if you please.

LITA

Did you know that we fight with Americanos, Donna Josefa? It's true. Just now they told me.

JOSEFA

Nuna, who brought this news?

NUNA

Santos.

JOSEFA

Bring him to me.

NUNA

He has gone to the village.

JOSEFA

Bring him . . . have him found. And stop that music. Tell them to take their wailing further away. Out now, all of you.

[*All go except* VERI *and* JOSEFA.]

VERI

Well, if it be so you're at least rid of him before you have to take second place in his house. The gringos spare no prisoners.

JOSEFA

Take out your ashes and beware you don't spill them!

VERI

In all humility, yes, madonna.

JOSEFA

What were you saying to the women?

VERI

I was only reminding them, since they are so young and so fat-brained, that the women of a country never change, Donna Josefa. Lo, if a mare but answer the bit softly and remember her paces, what matters a change of riders now and then?

JOSEFA

Empty your ashes.

VERI

Oh, it was nothing about madonna . . . not the lightest word.

JOSEFA

You have spoken too many covert insults about me, Veri. I'm not compelled to hear them.

VERI

No, truly? I was once in a position to repel insults myself, dear lady. I was his first love . . . his second bore him two sons . . . you are the third . . . and a fourth trembles now into his waiting arms. Bear insults, Josefa!

You will yet bear ashes like myself and Diana will give you orders.

JOSEFA

When I live to take her orders!

VERI

That was what I said! But I lived . . . and I took orders . . . even from you!
[FATHER MARTINEZ *has entered from within.*]

JOSEFA

[*Pointing*] Quick!
[VERI *goes through the outer door.*]

MARTINEZ

Good evening, Donna Josefa.

JOSEFA

Good evening, father. I was not aware that we had a guest.

MARTINEZ

I have only now come up the path . . . and I heard the women crying. . . .

JOSEFA

There's news of a battle . . .

MARTINEZ

Yes. Rumors have reached the village.

JOSEFA

A soldier was here . . . Santos.

MARTINEZ

He's below now . . . with a crowd around him.

JOSEFA

It's his story? That Pablo's a prisoner?

MARTINEZ

His among others.

JOSEFA

Do you believe it?

MARTINEZ

Remember this was a battle fought at night and in great confusion. Those who ran away would need a good story to tell.

JOSEFA

Yes . . . but it shakes one . . . it might happen.

MARTINEZ

Don't let their hysteria take hold on you. The peons are a credulous lot and their wives are worse. They believe the worst to avert misfortune. There'll be better news tonight.

JOSEFA

God send it soon.

MARTINEZ

Pablo Montoya is an old hand at mountain warfare. He's never been defeated or even checked. He's not the man to be beaten in a first skirmish, nor to be taken prisoner at any time.

JOSEFA

But suppose it were worse than that? What happens to you . . . or me . . . or to this house?

MARTINEZ

Worse than that? Wcrse than prisoner? Ask what would happen to Taos . . . and New Mexico? We are the farthest arm of an old civilization here. . . . We are rich, and there are great houses on our hills. . . . But there has been only one man of all the ricos who dared face the north and fight it. And that is your husband. He must return.

JOSEFA

And he will?

MARTINEZ

Yes . . . and he will.

JOSEFA

Only . . . you say that out of a great need to have it so.

MARTINEZ

Perhaps.

JOSEFA

And there's something else behind it.

MARTINEZ

No.

JOSEFA

Yes. You don't trust me. You know that if Pablo were dead there'd be some power in my hands. And you want to know what I'd do with it.

MARTINEZ

Would you answer such a question?

JOSEFA

Not till I know what power I'll have.

MARTINEZ

Let us be honest. It has occurred to you as well as to me that if Pablo were dead on the mountain, Federico would inherit his place and his power. Also that you are not much older than Federico . . . and he looks on you with friendly eyes.

JOSEFA

[*Angry*] If you were not a priest!

MARTINEZ

Forget who I am! When things happen one faces them!
You are Pablo's wife and Federico is his son. Never-
theless, if Pablo's dead you'll go to Federico. . . .

JOSEFA

You should have thought of that before you encour-
aged Pablo to set a new wife over me!

MARTINEZ

But I haven't, Josefa!

JOSEFA

You knew of it! He wouldn't go about it without telling
you! It's like him to pick out a slave I gave orders to,
and plan to make her mistress over me!

MARTINEZ

But I had no part in it. He will do as he pleases in this
as in other things. If any man could influence him I
might . . . but it was hopeless.

JOSEFA

Did you try?

MARTINEZ

I did. Not so much for you, it may be, but to keep his
weakness from the world. When we all depend so heavily
on one man it's dangerous to allow laughter at him. And
after all, he's sixty . . . she's not yet twenty. No matter how much power a man wields they always laugh a
little at that . . . in corners. . . .

JOSEFA

I had my laugh . . . but it was a bitter one.

MARTINEZ

His father was lord of life and death before him, and
he's been a god so long here in the valley that he thinks
he's a god in fact. That's his strength, too, though it
sometimes makes him a fool.

JOSEFA

I hate him! Hate him!

MARTINEZ

Well . . . that part of it's done. If he lives he's earned
your hatred. But if he's dead, what are we to do,
Josefa?

JOSEFA

It's not for me to decide.

MARTINEZ

Federico will decide it. Help me with that, Josefa! We cannot retreat . . . must not be defeated. Help me to hold Federico to what his father would have done!

JOSEFA

Father, if Pablo Montoya is dead on the mountain, it won't matter much who rules in Taos . . . or who influences the ruler! Federico could never hold back the Americanos. It's senseless to think so.

MARTINEZ

Montoya's son—

JOSEFA

And don't be misled about me! Much as I hate Montoya, I hate the Americanos more! May he live to kill them! I'll be a slave in his house if I must, with his new woman over me . . . but may he live to kill them! Does that answer you?

MARTINEZ

Josefa . . .
[DIANA, *a girl of eighteen, comes in, finds that she is intruding, and goes on toward the outer door.*]

DIANA

I'm sorry. I thought I heard someone calling. Was there news . . . of the battle?

JOSEFA

No. Nothing.

DIANA

Oh. [*She goes on.*]

MARTINEZ

There have been conflicting reports, Diana, but nothing we can count on.

DIANA

Thank you, father. [*She goes out.*]

JOSEFA

There walks his new lady, a skin with ten years less wear . . . and that's all she has.

MARTINEZ

I've always thought her a gentle child.

JOSEFA

Does a woman tempt without intending it? She'll be fat, though, fat before I am, and uglier when she's forty than I'll be at fifty.

MARTINEZ

And less faithful. He may discover that——

JOSEFA

That she loves Felipe?

MARTINEZ

You know that, too?

JOSEFA

Only that I've seen it in their eyes!

MARTINEZ

Felipe is his heart's darling, his stainless son. And Felipe loves the girl he intends to marry. I think this may make the marriage more than doubtful.

JOSEFA

No. He'd kill Felipe.

MARTINEZ

He'd be in no mood for marrying.
[*There is a sudden loud cry outside from the crowd of peons, then a silence followed by a babble of voices.* DIEGO, *a peon, enters.*]

DIEGO

Don Federico is returning!

MARTINEZ

Federico!

DIEGO

His troop is climbing the trail!

MARTINEZ

We'll know from him.

DIEGO

Excuse me, father! Excuse me, madonna. [*She runs out.*]

MARTINEZ

But you spoke truth concerning Pablo? You'd rather take a lower place in his household than see him defeated?

JOSEFA

If I can bear it! If I find I can bear it!

MARTINEZ

Then remember this, Donna Josefa: if he has been defeated, and we are never to see him again, we must still go on without him. Federico will have to step into his place. Whatever has happened, help me to keep up Federico's courage.

JOSEFA

I'll do what I can.

[FEDERICO *enters with* TWO SOLDIERS *and many women*

and peons listening for news. DIANA *slips in among them. The men are dressed in black buckskin, with silver buttons. Serapes are thrown over the soldiers' shoulders.* FEDERICO'S *hunting-shirt, however, is of white buckskin, the mark of the men of the* MONTOYA *family.*]

FEDERICO

Greetings, Donna Josefa . . . greetings, father!
We're back from the wars! Clear out of here, you trash!
Nobody's killed so far as I know, I tell you . . .
They ran like hell, the pack of them . . . they never
Got close enough to get killed! Get out! Get out!
[*The crowd clears out, the soldiers with them.* DIANA *goes toward the inner door.*]
Are we alone? The news is bad enough
In conscience. My father's dead. He was cut off
At the pass by a posse of trappers. We tried to reach him
But they were all massacred there. Keep this from the peons
Till something's decided. They may take to the hills
If they hear of it.

MARTINEZ

And so . . . Montoya's dead . . .

FEDERICO

We waited as long as there seemed any chance . . .

But these trappers take scalps like Indians; they
  wouldn't neglect
A trophy like Pablo Montoya's.

MARTINEZ

And how are we left?

FEDERICO

We're left as we always were . . . hanging on by our
  eye-lids.
They met us with five hundred men . . . we had,
Say, fifteen hundred. They were trappers with rifles
And a few troops . . . they've sworn to get revenge
For the massacre at Taos. The man who ordered
The American governor killed brought this on us
And we'll all pay for it . . . the ones who've paid
  already,
They're the lucky ones.

MARTINEZ

You were defeated?

FEDERICO

God love you!
What do you expect? Fifteen hundred with spears
And bows and arrows, and a few old-fashioned muskets
Go out to meet troops from the north, and trappers
  who hunt

For a living! Is it likely we'd win? If it hadn't been
    dark
With a heavy snow falling, just when it bothered them
    most
They'd be here now in possession, and we'd be hidden
Somewhere in the rocks with the catamounts.

MARTINEZ

And why?
If I may ask, are they not here, these victors?

FEDERICO

Because the snow sent them back. They hadn't counted
On two feet of snow in the trail, and they returned
To reorganize for the weather. But not for us,
Let me assure you. We didn't hinder them.

MARTINEZ

There's only one pass. You met them there?

FEDERICO

Holy father,
What's a pass to a trapper? They went around it, be-
    hind it
Under it, any way but through it . . . the troops
Tried a charge at the summit, and a few were killed,
But that was their only error.

JOSEFA

What can we do?

FEDERICO

Before they break through and exterminate us all
To pay us out in kind, someone who can speak
Had better speak for the valley, and speak quickly
While there's still time to negotiate.

MARTINEZ

Never.

FEDERICO

Well,
Perhaps you want to die, but I don't. Not yet.
The United States has formally taken over
This region of ours, and sent a governor . . .
We killed him and killed every northerner we could find
Along with him in Taos. Now vengeance may be
Delayed sometimes . . . bad weather can block the
    roads
And even cool the blood, but a governor
Was killed, and that's a first-rate challenge to
The northerners' sovereignty!

MARTINEZ

It was meant to be.

FEDERICO

Exactly . . . and it was . . . and they'll roll down
On us, like the mills of God. It may take time,
But it's sure as that . . . New Mexico is lost

To Spain and to Mexico, and to you and me.
It's as sure as death . . . and the only thing we can
    hope
To save out of it is our lives . . . if we're in time. . . .

MARTINEZ

You are the elder son
Of Pablo Montoya, Federico . . . it will be presumed
That you speak for Taos and New Mexico
In your father's absence . . . but before you speak
Give me a word with you in private.

FEDERICO

Surely . . .
Any number.

MARTINEZ

Now?

FEDERICO

When I've disposed
My troops and given a few last orders. Then
I shall be at your service. Give me this room alone
A little while, Josefa.

JOSEFA

Very well.
[MARTINEZ and DIANA go out.]

FEDERICO

I shan't need you, Narciso: Tell the men
To meet at dawn at the church for a muster call.
Till then they can sleep.

NARCISO

Yes, captain.

FEDERICO

And, on your way,
Send in the prisoner to me.
[NARCISO goes out.]

JOSEFA

I give you welcome,
And my love, Federico.

FEDERICO

Thank you, Josefa.

JOSEFA

No more?

FEDERICO

This is desperate business. I have no time.

JOSEFA

We have this moment.

FEDERICO

When I'm trying to snatch

Some safety from the wreck . . . bear this in mind,
We must not be seen together.

JOSEFA

When have I
Forgotten that?

FEDERICO

Also it's necessary
For both of us to forget whatever's past
Between you and me.

JOSEFA

And why?

FEDERICO

Because, for one thing,
You are my father's wife.

JOSEFA

You thought little of that
A day or two ago. And if, as you say,
Pablo is dead, there's less reason to think of it now.
What are you trying to think yourself into? What
  wrong
Have I done, that wasn't done me first? A woman
Has a right to any revenge she can take!

FEDERICO

That's true.
Take any revenge you can, then. But not with me.

JOSEFA

Why, yes . . . I see it. You're to be in power here . . .
And I'm not chosen. Not now. Who is it, then?
Who is it?

FEDERICO

No one.

JOSEFA

Diana? I think it is.
She's snared you too. I've seen you look after her . . .

FEDERICO

It's no one.

JOSEFA

It is Diana. May she burn
In hell, and all three with her!

FEDERICO

Will you go now?
[*An* OFFICER, *dressed as a trapper is brought to the door*
by TWO SOLDIERS.]
Leave him alone with me.
[JOSEFA *goes within. The* TWO SOLDIERS *go through
the outside door, closing it.* FEDERICO *closes the door
behind* JOSEFA.]
The devil's in these priests,
And the women, too.
What happened at the pass?

OFFICER

It worked as planned.

FEDERICO

And my father . . . ?

OFFICER

It's pretty certain.
There was nobody left alive there.

FEDERICO

You do your work thoroughly.

OFFICER

You weren't
Exactly in this for his health, were you? Be thankful
He's out of your way. He'd put you out of his
Fast enough.

FEDERICO

I know that. It can't be helped.
I'll have to go through with it.

OFFICER

Good. What is it you want?

FEDERICO

I want to govern Taos . . . with your guarantee.

OFFICER

You have little to offer.

FEDERICO

I've already given
More than you'll find it easy to repay.
You'd have walked into the old man's trap, and your
  nose
Would be two feet under snow if I hadn't stopped you.
Do you find that little?

OFFICER

No.
But that's done . . . that's past. We did win, and I
  think
You'll agree the war's over.

FEDERICO

And that's what a word of honor means to Americanos!
The war's over,
And whatever you promised is wiped out.

OFFICER

I don't say that . . .
But I do say, don't ask too much, don't hope
To get all your father had and our guarantee
Behind you to keep it. No one can guarantee
You'll keep your job if you muff it, also my powers

Are limited here. I'll be doing well for you
If I save your property for you, and that of your
  friends.
Or even part of it.

FEDERICO

Be on your way then!
If that's how much you trust me, and all you're trusted
At home, I've no more to say!

OFFICER

There's no use being touchy
And turning Castilian on me at this stage.
I can use you and you can use me, but kindly
Don't ask too much . . . or you'll ask more than I've
  got
And you'll get nothing. This is the way we stand:
Taos has been defeated, and Taos is due
To be ground under. You murdered our governor
And very likely you'll have to produce a scape-goat
To stand the gaff for that. But when that's over
We'll want somebody in power here that understands
The peons and the ricos . . . and you could have it
And keep your father's property to boot
If you're willing to take orders, and keep order among
Your aristocratic friends.

FEDERICO

Oh, I'm to take orders.

OFFICER

You're damn right you'll take orders! You'll be glad
Of the chance to live unmolested on your land.
You've had it soft here, you and your class. Your peons
Jump when you speak. The king of Spain couldn't ask
More than your father got in the way of service.
But that's all past. Times change. But I'll save your
    ranch,
And my price for this is exactly half your holdings.

FEDERICO

Half my land?

OFFICER

I could take all, but I leave you half of it,
Being generous to a fault.

FEDERICO

A Yankee peddler . . .
That's what I have to deal with!

OFFICER

I could make it
Two-thirds, now I've been insulted, but I won't,
I'll stick to half.

FEDERICO

And I'd live neighbor to you
And see you lining your nest with what you've stolen.
No, by God, I can't do that!

OFFICER

I have no more desire to live next door
To you than you to me. I won't live here.
I'll put an agent in charge.

FEDERICO

Why, then, I'll take it. . . .
Provided I don't have to see you again.

OFFICER

Good. Then . . .
You'll be willing to sign this paper before I go.

FEDERICO

[*Reading it*]
No, I will not. This takes the house from me.

OFFICER

Sign it, my good lad, sign it . . . and I'll try hard
To save the estate from appropriation by
The new governor. Your father was a rebel
Against our government, and his land's forfeit . . .
    yes,

All of it . . . but I think I can save it.

FEDERICO

[*He sits down and signs the paper*]
If I'd known what this would come to you could all be
    damned.
And I'd go with you, before I'd touch this!

OFFICER

I swear I've done you a favor. One more thing. . . .
I want a map of this place.

FEDERICO

What place?

OFFICER

The estate. . . .
I want to know what I've got. It's a peddler's no-
    tion . . .
But I want to see it.

FEDERICO

There is none.

OFFICER

Draw one then. . . .
I want to see it.
[FEDERICO *goes to a case near the fireplace, takes out
papers and brings a map. The* OFFICER *looks at it.*]
How many acres in all?

FEDERICO

Eighteen thousand.

OFFICER

Why, that's enough for both,
Plenty for both. I'll take this with me, and have
A copy made.

FEDERICO

I may need it.

OFFICER

I'll bring it back,
Or another just as good, showing your half.
You see I'm a man of my word. I stick to half.
Do you want the place you're offered?

FEDERICO

I'll take it.

OFFICER

Remember
This is no child's play. If you show any sign
Of treachery . . . and you'll be watched . . . you go
By a quick route. You won't be popular
With the new citizens you'll have.

FEDERICO

I know. . . .
And better than you can tell me, what's left to me,
And what my place will be.

OFFICER

Get the ricos out then. . . .
See to it there's no resistance, or not enough
To make us trouble, and I'll do my part. . . .

FEDERICO

Well, I'll do mine.
You'll find me here alone when you march on Taos.

OFFICER

Goodnight, then.

FEDERICO

Goodnight.
[*He leads to the inner door.*]
Go this way. The small door there sharp to your right.
It leads to an alley-way, and that will take you
To a little gate. Open it. There's a path
Straight down the hill.
[*The* OFFICER *goes out.* FEDERICO *returns to the table.
The women have begun their wailing song again out-
side.* FEDERICO *listens for a moment, then makes a
gesture of impatience and strikes a bell.* GRASO *enters.*]

GRASO

Yes, senor.

FEDERICO

Tell them to take that tune of theirs further away.
What's the matter with them now?

GRASO

Some of your men, senor, brought confirmation of
deaths, and the women are mourning.

FEDERICO

They'll have to do their mourning outside the plaza
tonight. I've heard too much of it. Tell them that.

GRASO

Yes, senor. Also Don Hermano and Don Miguel have
returned and wish to speak with you.

FEDERICO

Let them come in.
[GRASO *goes out.* FATHER MARTINEZ *enters from
within.*]

MARTINEZ

We've seen many torches across the valley, Federico.
They were near Don Hermano's hacienda.

FEDERICO

He's here,
And Don Miguel with him.

MARTINEZ

Good. They may perhaps help me
With what I wanted to say. I wanted to see you

Before you were committed to a course
Toward the Americanos.

FEDERICO

It doesn't follow, you know,
That because I'm my father's son, I'll do as he did,
Or that his friends will be mine.

MARTINEZ

I have no wish
To be an inherited friend.
But if we can help each other, why not?

FEDERICO

I doubt
That you can help me. If, in any way,
I can help you . . . why, speak.
[DON HERMANO *and* DON MIGUEL *enter. They are
ricos, proudly dressed.*]

HERMANO

You're here before us,
Don Federico.

FEDERICO

You're welcome, Don Hermano,
And you, Don Miguel.
[*They embrace.*]

MIGUEL

Thank you. Now, God be praised.
There's one Montoya here!

HERMANO

No word of your father?

FEDERICO

None.

MIGUEL

Nor of Felipe?

FEDERICO

Yes, he was seen
After the battle.

HERMANO

He'll be with us then,
And that will help. Good-evening, father.

MARTINEZ

Good-evening,
Don Hermano . . . and to you, Don Miguel . . .
I saw the lights around your gates and found them
Most reassuring.
[*They bow to* MARTINEZ, *who returns the salutation.*]

MIGUEL

It was reassuring to be there . . .
And to find I had some neighbors left.

MARTINEZ

You led your men home with you?

MIGUEL

What remained of them.
There were some missing. Hermano overtook me
And brought me along. . . . We mean to see this
   through.

HERMANO

Whatever we do we must do together now. . . .

MARTINEZ

I knew we could count on you.

HERMANO

And whatever has happened
To Pablo Montoya . . . we pledge ourselves, and I
   think
We can pledge all the ricos that return,
To stay with you to the end.

MIGUEL

It's touch and go;
We must face that, for Montoya was our man. . . .
But if there's still Federico to lead them, and they
Aren't given a moment to think, or consult their wives,

We can herd them into one last dash, and catch
The Americans off their guard.

FEDERICO

It might be done.

HERMANO

Can you think of a better way?

FEDERICO

I can think of nothing
That won't be fatal in the end.

HERMANO

You'd surrender?

FEDERICO

No.
What good would it do to surrender? We're under
    death sentence . . .
All of us if we stay here.

MARTINEZ

Suppose your father
Were now alive, what plan would he follow?

FEDERICO

If you
Are fortunate enough to know, why answer?

MARTINEZ

The Yankees
Are on the way back to Sante Fe. They find it
Rather hard going. They'll be camped tonight
Not far from where you met them. At the pass.
They'll be cold and sleep sound, and keep a poor guard,
Not having much discipline. They're at your mercy.
Your father'd be there before morning.

FEDERICO

And suppose we slaughtered four
Or five hundred, and the rest got away
To tell the story, well, then, what have we gained?
Only another massacre to set
Against our names and rouse the Americans.

MARTINEZ

They wouldn't march so readily this way
Next time, if they left five hundred men on the hills.

FEDERICO

Are you honest in this, and crazy, or cunning and sane?
You have a brain, you must know, if you lie awake
And think in the night, that we can't win over a nation.
We're a broken end of an empire here, cut off
And dying. . . . Mexico's a republic, and we're
Disowned at Mexico City. The United States

Has men and arms and armies. Do you want to die?
Have you set your heart on dying?

MARTINEZ

No.

FEDERICO

Well, then
You must be cunning . . . you must see your way
To send me against the north to wreak your vengeance
While you escape, and let the rest of us pay.
My father's paid already. . . .

MARTINEZ

Your father needed
No urging.

FEDERICO

Then you're innocent of his death.
But it's still true that you knew when he went
That it was hopeless . . . you knew when the massacre
Was planned that it would all turn out as it has. . . .
You knew they'd send an army against us then
And we couldn't stop it. . . .

MARTINEZ

It seems to have stopped. . . .

FEDERICO

Not for long!

If it took them a hundred years they'd have to wipe out
The blood that was spilled here. . . .

MARTINEZ

Are you so sure
The north will beat us?

FEDERICO

I wish I were as sure
Of living through the next year, as I am of that.
Beat us? Our hundreds against their millions?
Our muskets against their rifles! Beat us!

MARTINEZ

When
Your father was alive, would you have dared
To tell him that?

FEDERICO

What's that to do with it?

MARTINEZ

This: the reason you couldn't tell him then
Was that it wasn't true then. While he was alive
We couldn't be conquered. Yes, while there was one
In this whole region that would not bow, they were
   helpless
To set up their sovereignty—here.

FEDERICO

They set it up.

MARTINEZ

And he tore it down! The strength
Of a state is not in its numbers but in faith.
I have seen your father stand at the plaza gate
And look out over the valley . . . and every peon
Looking up from the fields, and every neighbor
On the adjoining hills, knew while he stood there,
Stood firm and would not falter, their world was safe;
The rulers to the north
Knew that, and when they had to make a gesture,
Urged on by those behind, they made it slyly,
Reluctantly and in fear! This governor
They sent out over us, he was a man of straw
Set up to try the wind and see how much
We could be made to endure. We endured nothing.
Pablo Montoya turned on them. They died
Before an order was issued.

FEDERICO

And Pablo Montoya
Is also dead.

MARTINEZ

Even so, they've retreated.
Even so, I feel all about us still the spirit
Of Pablo Montoya. His courage

Is over us like a mantle, and it falls
Inevitably to your shoulders.

FEDERICO

No.

MARTINEZ

But it does!
Take up the lance he dropped, call on us to follow. . . .
Believe in us and our cause and the great days
We've lived through in the past, and this enemy
You think so well of dissolves to a rabble before you
And lets you through! The man who is his son
Has greatness in him! Wherever he went
He carried with him the center of an age,
The center of a culture, and people's hearts
Clung to him like vines to rock! You, too, are this
    man . . .
His other self, his heir . . . all eyes are on you. . . .
When you are in your house the people will say . . .
He is in his house, we are secure . . . he thinks for
    us. . . .
We can sleep tonight. When you ride on a journey
The people's gaze will go with you anxiously . . .
And scan the horizon for your return! But beware,
If you betray this.

FEDERICO

Yes . . . he was such a man . . .

And I might be.
[*He rises.*]
Even tonight, even now,
I could strike at them. . . .

MIGUEL

You could do more than strike.
You could finish them . . . make an end to them.

FEDERICO

No.
[*The thought of his bargain has come back on him.*]

HERMANO

Think . . .
Think what we have to lose. Nowhere on this earth
Will we find a life like ours, or ever again
Live as we live here. Ours is a little clan.
But we stem from a great nation; this is worth defending
From gringos who have nothing.

FEDERICO

Is he padre or wizard . . .
To turn the truth inside out? We're struck to the heart,
And the wound's mortal. It's too late for courage.
You know it as well as I.

MIGUEL

Too late! We've fought
One indecisive battle!

FEDERICO

Too late because
We're out of fashion! Our guns are out of fashion,
Also our speech and our customs and our blood.
They're the new race with the new weapons!

MIGUEL

We must fight them or die.

FEDERICO

We can retreat.

HERMANO

And abandon Taos to them?

MARTINEZ

Is that your counsel . . .
To abandon Taos?

FEDERICO

I can think of nothing better.

MIGUEL

I believe you mean this.

FEDERICO

I do.
[*A pause.*]

MIGUEL

Why, then, let's go.
I had some hope when I came here.

FEDERICO

Don't think I'm happy
To say this to you. I like it no more than you do.

HERMANO

No . . . but to leave our houses, our flocks, to turn
The peons adrift. . . . I'd rather make a stand
And die for it. And you would!

FEDERICO

No. I would not.

MIGUEL

Will you go now?

HERMANO

Yes. Goodnight, Don Federico.

FEDERICO

Goodnight, Don Hermano. Goodnight, Don Miguel.

MIGUEL

Goodnight.

FEDERICO

What are your plans?

HERMANO

I have none. We'll need
No plans for what's left to do.
[DON HERMANO *and* DON MIGUEL *go out.*]

MARTINEZ

And what are yours?
If I may ask.

FEDERICO

To salvage what I can carry.

MARTINEZ

What can one carry that's of any value?
What we have is Taos. Losing our city,
We have nothing left. . . .
[NUNA *comes to the door, bringing* SANTOS.]

FEDERICO

If you'll pardon me,
I have much to do.

NUNA

Is Donna Josefa here?

FEDERICO

[*Stepping toward the inner door*] What do you want?

NUNA

[*Frightened*] She sent me for Santos.

FEDERICO

Must you track through the hall? [*He goes through the inner door.*]

NUNA

She was here . . . she sent . . . He's angry at me.

MARTINEZ

She may have sent you, dear child, but you are obviously not wanted now. Nor I either, you might add. . . . Come along, and bring Santos with you.
[*He goes through the outer door.* DIANA *enters from within.*]

NUNA

Senorita!

DIANA

Yes.

NUNA

Is Donna Josefa within?

DIANA

I don't know.

NUNA

She sent me. . . . I was to bring old Santos. . . .

DIANA

Nunita, tell me . . . can you be true . . . and silent?

NUNA

Yes, senorita. . . .

DIANA

Could you be a friend to me?

NUNA

But I am a servant. . . . I'll be your servant.

DIANA

No . . . it's more than that. If I ask you a question, you'll never tell that I asked it?

NUNA

Never.

DIANA

Then . . . tell me. . . . Is Senor Felipe alive?

NUNA

Yes, senorita, they think so.

DIANA

But they're not certain?

NUNA

No.

DIANA

He'd be back if he were alive . . . don't they say
that? . . . I thought I heard them say that, from a
window. . . .

NUNA

He's late coming, but that might be. Santos?

DIANA

No . . . no!

NUNA

I'll be careful. Santos . . .
[SANTOS *comes forward.*]

SANTOS

Yes, Nunita.

NUNA

Did anyone go back along the pass to look at the faces
of the slain?

SANTOS

No, no, it was dangerous. You could not.

NUNA

But if any were wounded . . . they would be cared for?

SANTOS

Girl, how can I tell? . . . Am I not brought here to speak with the Donna Josefa?

NUNA

You speak with Senorita Diana, pig, and she is even greater than Donna Josefa!

SANTOS

Is she indeed? I did not know. [*He takes off his cap.*]

NUNA

The senorita wishes to know if the wounded of Taos will be cared for.

SANTOS

Ah, that is with God!

NUNA

One can see that it is not with Santos.

SANTOS

But senorita!

NUNA

Would you go back along that trail for her?

SANTOS

But when one has escaped by miracle with his life would he tempt the good God by returning?

NUNA

Our Santos is afraid . . . afraid of Americanos!

SANTOS

No. . . . No! Who would be afraid of Americanos? They are a small and weak nation, compared with the people of Taos . . . but they have rifles, and rifles are deadly.

NUNA

Then that's all, Santos. . . .

SANTOS

But the Donna Josefa . . .

NUNA

She won't see you today.

SANTOS

If I have incurred displeasure . . .

DIANA

No . . . no . . . only that's all now.
[SANTOS *withdraws, cringing.*]

NUNA

But I would go.

DIANA

Where?

NUNA

Back along the trail.

DIANA

We'd never find it. . . . You'd go with me?

NUNA

Yes.

DIANA

We'd never find it.

NUNA

No, it's true. We wouldn't. It's dark and cold . . . and a long way.

DIANA

Only . . . there are men lying there at this moment.

NUNA

You love him?

DIANA

No! . . . say nothing of this! . . . run away! . . . Oh, Nuna, Nuna. . . . I can't talk to you . . . nor to anyone . . . but you know what hangs over me.

NUNA

I know. We have all heard.

DIANA

And what do the women say?

NUNA

They say you're lucky mostly.

DIANA

He may be dead.

NUNA

They say he is . . . and they say Felipe's alive.

DIANA

Oh, God . . . if that could be true!
[VERI *enters carrying linen through.*]

VERI

You're wanted, Nuna. [*She goes up to* DIANA.] And
this is the piece of flesh he had in his eye. This is his dish.
[*She pulls* DIANA's *shawl away from her breast.*] Curds
and cream for the old goat!

NUNA

Let her alone!
[*She drags* VERI *away.*]

VERI

From what I hear he'll keep warm with the jackals to-night . . . not with my lady.

DIANA

What have you against me, Veri?

VERI

That he should want you . . . that's all!

NUNA

You'd better go make those beds!

VERI

Before God, this one's putting on airs now . . . and she's pretty, too. She'll be marrying Don Federico and running the house. Well . . . when it happens remember I spat on you once . . . pht!
[*She goes in.* NUNA *is grave for a moment, then is unable to restrain a smile.*]

NUNA

Forgive me.
[*A loud clear voice is heard outside calling a name,* "*Felipe!*".]

MARTINEZ

[*Outside*] Now God be praised . . . Felipe! It is Felipe!

LIBRARY ASSOCIATION
... OF ...
PORTLAND ORE

FELIPE

[*Outside*] Good evening, father. It's Felipe. You're not mistaken.

MARTINEZ

[*Outside*] Wounded?

FELIPE

[*Outside*] Enough to hurt. That's all.
[DIANA *sits.*]

MARTINEZ

[*Outside*] Let me see.

FELIPE

[*Outside*] I'm well.

MARTINEZ

[*Outside*] You come late.
[FELIPE *and* MARTINEZ *enter.*]

FELIPE

I went back over the ground to look for my father;
We found some dead and some dying; on both
    sides . . .
But not the man we were looking for.
[NUNA *goes out backwards, all eyes.*]

MARTINEZ

He was gone.

FELIPE

He must be dead, or wounded too badly to answer.
We called his name . . . and I got this scratch for my
  pains.
Some of the trappers shot at us from the rocks,
Where they'd taken shelter. It's a moonless night,
And the snow fell so fast the bodies were covered
Before we reached them. And yet I can't believe
He's there among them.

MARTINEZ

I hope not!

FELIPE

I hope not. Good evening, senorita.

DIANA

Good evening, senor.

FELIPE

Federico's returned?

DIANA

Yes, unwounded.

FELIPE

I must speak to him.
I came upon real panic in the village.

They've heard of my father's death, but they're not
    mourning.
They've put away their guitars, and the burros
Are loaded for a flight to the mountains. Look, from
    that window.
You can see the lights of lanterns in the street
Gathering like fireflies. When these people are silent
They're badly frightened.

MARTINEZ

Federico's here.
I'll tell him you've come.
[*He goes within.*]

FELIPE

Diana.

DIANA

Yes. Yes, senor.

FELIPE

I break a bond with myself when I speak to you
Alone. I've sworn I would not.

DIANA

Yes . . . I've known it.

FELIPE

But now we have only a moment, and whether we'll ever
Be given another . . .

[*He breaks off.*]
Should my father not return
You'll have enemies here. . . .

DIANA

Yes.

FELIPE

Count on me to help you
In any way I can.

DIANA

Then . . . he won't return?

FELIPE

I did what I could to find him. If he were alive
It seems there'd have been some trace . . . or a hint
  somewhere.
Yet in my heart I think he lives.

DIANA

And I . . .
I think so.

FELIPE

Why, Diana?

DIANA

Because I fear it.

FELIPE

I'm sorry . . . I fear . . . the other.

DIANA

If he
Had failed to see me, I could have loved him too.

FELIPE

What plans we can make for you should be made at
    once.
I think they'll lay this valley desolate. . . .
The Americans . . . and those of us whose lot
Is cast with Taos will go with our city. But you
Have northern blood in your veins . . . you came here
    by chance,
A prisoner . . . and there's no reason why you should
    add
One life more to the slaughter. There must be some way
To send you where you'll be safe, and can find friends
Before the worst happens. That much I can do.

DIANA

Do you want me away?

FELIPE

I want you to be safe.

DIANA

And you stay here to be killed?

FELIPE

That's the price one pays

For being a Montoya in Taos. There's no such reason
Why you should remain. . . . Diana . . . if this were
  said . . .
This that's between us . . . if it were ever in words
You'd be mine in my heart . . . not his . . . I'd go
  mad
To take you in my arms . . . and it would be mad-
  ness. . . .
Because I'd want him dead . . . my father . . . the
  man
I've loved and honored above all others . . . and still
Do love and honor.

DIANA

If you must die with Taos . . .
Felipe, Felipe!

FELIPE

Try not to say it!

DIANA

Then I . . .
I must die here too.

FELIPE

So long as one loves
In silence it can be borne . . . as much as before
My father stands between us.

DIANA

Not if he's dead!

FELIPE

But he's not . . . I feel it and know it. He'll be here
And take you from me. And how can I bear that now,
Now that I know? I should have left this house
And stayed away till it all burned out . . . but that
Was impossible . . . so I lived here, and loved you
      more
And fought against it. But always when I saw you
It's been the same.

DIANA

I'm glad.

FELIPE

We know it now.
We must be content with that.

DIANA

But don't ask me to go.

FELIPE

You're the one thing in my world
I can save out of it, and I must save it. You'd be
A needless sacrifice.

DIANA

It's all needless, Felipe,
Needless and useless for you as well as for me.
You must not die, Felipe.

FELIPE

But there's one thing
A man can't do . . .

DIANA

What is it?

FELIPE

Desert in danger.
I'm my father's son, Diana. We have a strict code.
I can't break with it, nor with him. I'm a Spaniard,
And I honor my line and my name.

DIANA

But if all here
Are to die?

FELIPE

Yes, even if he
Were dead, and I knew it, I couldn't leave Taos. Not
If I were to keep respect for myself and believe
Myself worth saving. But I could wish I'd been born
In the north like you! . . . Then I'd say, let all the
    rest
Go where they like . . . let Taos and the Rio Grande
Dissolve like a mist and leave me fatherless
Alone by a strange river . . . if you'd come with me!
In the north no questions are asked; a man and a maid
May come and go as they like. We could make our own
    kingdom

Somewhere among them.

DIANA

And this defeat could mean freedom!

FELIPE

Yes.

DIANA

Felipe!

FELIPE

Yes?

DIANA

To think and act . . .
To love as one wills . . . to speak and walk like a
    queen
Freely in a free land . . . to love where we love
And no one to forbid us. Why, that's no kingdom,
Felipe, it's heaven!

FELIPE

Heaven we can never have.

DIANA

Are those the ways of the north?

FELIPE

Yes.

DIANA

And young
And old go their own paths, and no one is bound
To love except from his heart?

FELIPE

Yes.

DIANA

If these are my people,
And their blood is mine, and their ways are better
    than these,
Could you not live by them?

FELIPE

No.

DIANA

He's dead, Felipe.
And all this is dead around us . . . dead or dying . . .
He would have taken me from you when I loved
    you. . . .
Would still if he were here!

FELIPE

If Taos is dying
Put your love elsewhere, Diana, for I'm part of
    Taos . . .
And my blood's strong in me. You look abroad and see
The earth as a maze of many roads and cities,

All open to you . . . and yours to choose . . . but I
Am born to one world, and share its destiny
Whether it's good or bad. If my father's dead
I still belong to Taos. It's not a choice.
It's the only thing I can do.

DIANA

Then I have no choice.
I'll stay here with you.

FELIPE

You'd do that . . . to be near me?

DIANA

I have no more choice than you.

FELIPE

Diana, if
I put my arms once round you, I'll lose all sense
Of what I have to do . . .
[*He goes to her and takes her in his arms.*]
And so I lose it.

DIANA

There's someone watching.
[*She draws away from him.* FEDERICO, JOSEFA *and*
MARTINEZ *enter from within.*]

JOSEFA

Give them your blessing, father. She takes them
  all . . .
Our chaste Diana! Father, sons, Holy Ghost. . . .

FEDERICO

Be silent! Greetings, Felipe.

FELIPE

Greetings, brother.

FEDERICO

You're wounded.

FELIPE

It's not a wound. It's not that much.
[*The brothers embrace.*]

FEDERICO

Well . . . we've come out of this.

FELIPE

In some fashion or other.

FEDERICO

Yes . . . not too luckily . . .
Not with our father gone.

FELIPE

I looked for him.

FEDERICO

It was useless?

FELIPE

No one had seen him.
No one knew what had happened to him. And still
I'm certain somehow he is alive.

FEDERICO

If he were alive we'd have heard from him.
We'll have to get on without him.

FELIPE

If he were dead
The world would be one thing . . . but if he returns
Something quite different. Whatever plans we make
Must fit with both.

FEDERICO

My plans do fit with both.
[NARCISO *enters with a* SOLDIER.]

NARCISO

Don Federico, pardon me . . . I think you're needed
Below . . . they're panic-stricken, both men and
    women. . . .

FELIPE

When I came through the village the peons were pack-
    ing

And ready to leave for the range. You must make some
    announcement
Or they'll walk out from under us. Just now it looks
Like the flight into Egypt down there . . . on a vast
    scale. . . .
Only the Josephs are mounted on the donkeys
And the Marys are walking behind.

FEDERICO

There's no danger tonight,
Go down and quiet them, Narciso. Tell them
I'll give them a leader, and let them go before morning.

NARCISO

They won't believe me. The town's a caravan.

FEDERICO

Wait then. I'll go down and talk to them.

FELIPE

You'll give them
A leader . . . and let them go?

FEDERICO

I mean to stay here
With a few friends who've made their minds up to
    it. . . .

And stand the attack when it comes. They'll over-run
us,
Of course, but someone must stay behind to delay
them,
And to wait for Pablo. He might come. The peons
And those who wish to live are to take the trail
And make their escape. I give you charge of that.

FELIPE

You ask me to lead them?

FEDERICO

Yes.

FELIPE

That's a hard sentence . . .
To lead a retreat from Taos at a time
When men are needed here.

FEDERICO

Brother, men are needed
Most, where they'll do most good. If we all stay
The siege might be prolonged, but it would end
Exactly the same way. You're younger than I am
And it's better that you should live and use what tal-
ents
You have to find new lands for the citizens
And slaves who are driven out.

FELIPE

This may be necessary . . .
But not till we know what's happened to our father.

FEDERICO

You'll wait till morning, and then set out.

FELIPE

I don't like it.
It's a coward's job. If the peons must stampede,
Let them go. The fight's as much mine as yours.

FEDERICO

Brother, if we had one chance of holding out,
I'd say try it . . . all of us . . . but since it's hope-
    less
Before we start, I forbid it. It's noble to die,
No doubt, when you have a noble cause to die for,
But when you have no cause, when your cause is lost,
The fewer lives lost the better.

FELIPE

I don't like the role you
Cast me for. Lead the retreat yourself,
And leave me in Taos.

FEDERICO

No.

FELIPE

But I can say no
As well as you, Federico. I won't go.

FEDERICO

I've made it a command.

FELIPE

I don't understand you, Federico.
It's not like you to insist so firmly on dying . . .
Forgive me for saying so.

FEDERICO

Don't puzzle about it.
I have my reasons for wanting you out of the house,
And our father would have them if he were here.
You say he's alive and will return. If he does
He'll ask for Diana. I'd rather not have to tell him
To look for her with you.

FELIPE

And that's your reason?

MARTINEZ

These orders of yours fit oddly with what you told me
A while ago, Federico. You said, I believe,
That others might die if they cared to, defending Taos,
But you'd rather not.

FEDERICO

It may be I've changed my mind.

MARTINEZ

I don't think so. I think as Felipe does
That there's something odd about it.

FEDERICO

By God, he'll go,
Or I won't answer for him!

FELIPE

This is strange talk
For a brother, Federico.

FEDERICO

And you have strange manners
With the woman betrothed to your father! You're to go
And Diana stays here.

FELIPE

And now I quite understand you.
You mean to make peace and save what's left for your-
    self. . . .

FEDERICO

You're a little mad, I think, to make such a charge,
Mad with love, no doubt. Diana belongs
To Pablo Montoya, and he may return!

Meanwhile, to guard her honor, the least I can ask
Is that you take the road.

JOSEFA

He lies, Felipe.
He's done all this for Diana. Now strike at me!
But it's the truth!

FELIPE

You hear?

FEDERICO

Are we to listen
To women? My charge against you is just, and you
Retort with another. It's you who've been traitor-
    ous. . . .
But I've given you a chance for life. Will you take
    command
Of the expedition to the south, as I've ordered you,
Or are you an enemy?

FELIPE

I don't trust you.

FEDERICO

Arrest him. . . .
Arrest him, Narciso.

MARTINEZ

You anticipate a little,
Federico. You're not yet master here.

FEDERICO

You'll wait
A long time for another. Arrest him!

MARTINEZ

Narciso!
Mind what you do!

FEDERICO

If you ask for it I'll find
A way to quiet you, too! I need no priest's leave
For taking what I want. If I remain
Your master here, Diana is mine to give
And I take her for myself.

FELIPE

Yes?

FEDERICO

Let her learn to love
Where she finds it necessary. As things stand you've
   nothing
To offer her, and I have!
[NARCISO *approaches* FELIPE.]

FELIPE

[*Brushing him aside*]
May God pardon me.
[*He draws his sword.*]

FEDERICO

Lay your hands on him!

FELIPE

Give me fair play! You're not my father's son. . . .
I won't believe it!
[FEDERICO *draws*.]

FEDERICO

Let him alone, then! I warn you!
You're a novice at this business! I've made you an
    offer,
And you'd be wise to take it!

FELIPE

I'll take nothing!
[*The swords clash.* MARTINEZ *leaps between them,
catches the blades under his arm and breaks* FEDERICO's
sharp off. FEDERICO *drops the useless weapon and
draws his dagger.* FELIPE *tosses his sword back over
his shoulder and draws his dagger also. They manoeuver
for position slowly and silently.*]

FEDERICO

Narciso!

NARCISO

Yes!
[*He draws his sword and springs to* FEDERICO's *side.*

FELIPE *stoops and picks up his sword. There is a sudden sharp shout in unison from a distance:* "Montoya! Pablo Montoya!" *After a pause this is repeated:* "Montoya! Pablo Montoya!"]

MARTINEZ

That comes from the village! Wait!

FEDERICO

What are they saying?

THE CROWD

Montoya! Pablo Montoya!

MARTINEZ

They're calling Pablo Montoya!

JOSEFA

He's returned!

FELIPE

Yes. He's returned.

DIANA

[*At the window*]
They're coming up from the village . . . along the road.
[*She looks at* FELIPE, *and he at her. There is a silence, then* THE CROWD *can be heard singing.*]

FEDERICO

If he has come back we'll say no more about this.
[FELIPE *looks at him without answering.*]
You've made a groundless charge against me, Felipe,
And I was angry. But I'm willing to forget it
If you are.

FELIPE

What do you think it matters to me
Who you've betrayed or when?
[*He goes quickly to* DIANA *and bends over her.*]

MARTINEZ

We shall all do well,
I think, to forget whatever passed in this room.
[*The singing becomes audible again as* THE CROWD
*rounds a corner of the hills, and a patter of feet is
heard.* CONCHITA *comes in hurriedly.*]

CONCHITA

[*Breathless*]
It's . . . he's come!

MARTINEZ

Yes . . . we're waiting for him.
[*The singing stops and nothing is heard save the
trampling of feet.* TWO *or* THREE WOMEN *come to the
door and edge in silently. They are followed by* BOYS
and MEN. *The stage is filled, all looking back at the*

doorway as they pause. PABLO MONTOYA *enters, a solid,
burning-eyed man of sixty, his hair gray, his face in-
tent. He stops to take in the room, then comes to the
center.* OTHERS *enter behind him.* MONTOYA'S *glance
lights up as he sees* FELIPE. *He lays a hand on his arm
and then turns toward* FEDERICO *to greet him also.
But he stops when he notices the broken sword.*]

MONTOYA

Whose sword was that?

FEDERICO

Mine, Pablo.

MONTOYA

Take it up! It offends me! If swords must be broken
Let them break in a gringo's throat, against the bone,
Not in our houses!
[FEDERICO *picks up the sword.* MONTOYA *looks round
the room again.*]
Men of Taos, I have come home, and I bring
Only a doubtful victory. Women of Taos,
What victory we have, little though it is,
Has saved us from slavery, and those we must thank
    for that
Lie now on the mountains. They chose rather to die
Than live not free. First, let us mourn for them.
Mourn with me, women of Taos. They were my friends,

And your heart-break's mine. But our mourning must
  be brief,
And forgotten in anger. Let the women go out.
All save Diana.
[*The women go.*]
This was no defeat! We were betrayed at the pass,
Betrayed from within. If that were not so
We'd have spilled them like water, and not one death
Would have been needed!

HERMANO

Betrayed!

MONTOYA

Just that!
I went back over their march. They'd followed the trail
Through every pass till they came to the one where
  we waited. . . .
And then they went round to attack our flank! They
  knew
Where we were waiting for them! I read the story
There in the snow. It was plain. And somewhere among
  us
Some Indian-livered dog-spawn crouches that traded
Our plans to the north! Yes, by our God, and I'll find
  him
Before this night's out! If he stands here and hears me
Let him breathe deep, and taste the air! It's good,
This mountain air . . . and it's the last he'll have!

It happens I've taken an opportune prisoner or so,
And I know how to make them talk! We'll have that
   vengeance
Before we strike again!

HERMANO

We attack tomorrow?

MONTOYA

This was no victory for the Americans,
Remember! They had our plans . . . they attacked
   from the flank!
Where they knew we were unprepared. And they came
   to punish
The people of Taos. Instead we've crippled them
And sent them limping home! Punish Taos! They go
   back
To Santa Fe without seeing Taos! They left
Their own dead too on the mountain, and they'll look
   twice
Before they leap at our throats again! Why, look . . .
This was no defeat . . . but a victory that will lead
To victory again! They'll never touch Taos. . . .
They'll never push us back . . . no . . . rather we
Will push them out of Santa Fe, and northward
Back to their English mothers! We'll pledge to that.
Let each man pour himself a glass of wine,

And fill it full, for we drink death to the Yankees!
[*The men fill their glasses.*]
But before we drink we must know what more we drink
  to.
My ears are good. I have heard it said here and there
That Spain is old and I am old, and the dogs
Of the north will have their day. Do you believe this?
[*There is a slight pause, then a murmur of* "no, no,"
"no, no."]
And if you did what place would you have in the world?
None. You'd be the dogs of slaves, you'd be
The slaves of dogs. We come of an old, proud race,
From that part of the earth where the blood runs hot,
  and the hearts
Of men are resentful of insult. We are either lords
And masters of ourselves, or else we die.
And who are these conquerors who intend to take
Our places and our rights? For this is our place,
We wrought it out of a desert, built it up
To beauty and use; we live here well, we have
Customs and arts and wisdom handed down
To us through centuries. They would break this up,
And scatter it, these tricksters from the north.
They come here penniless, homeless, living with squaws
For women, vagabond barbarians, with hardly
A language, no laws, no loyalty . . . traders . . .
  whatever
They have they'll sell . . . behind each other's backs

They've sold me a thousand rifles! And I have them!
And when next we fight you'll use them.
[*The men lean forward.*]
And are these the men
To lop off an arm of Spain? Oh, brothers in blood,
If you are proud, take pride now in what we are!
It is said that Spain has abandoned us here, that we
live
Cut off from allegiance . . . under an ancient banner
That's lost its meaning . . . but Spain has never gone
back!
It's now three long centuries since Cortes led
His hundreds into Mexico. Had you listened
Then, you'd have heard Spain's enemies whisper-
ing. . . .
She spreads too far, her power will weaken soon. . . .
We'll wait . . . then strike! They waited a hundred
years. . . .
Then struck at Brazil! Two hundred years ago,
That was! And Spain roused and shook them off, and
ran
The Dutch from her colonies, and invaded Flanders
And wrote on their doors with blood! And if you had
listened
Behind those doors you'd have heard them whispering
again:
Wait! Spain is old . . . she has endured too long. . . .
We'll strike a little later! And they did wait.

Two hundred years they waited before Napoleon
Dared cross the border, and lost Europe crossing it!
And again they say Spain is old . . . she's ruled too
    long,
These stragglers from the north! She has ruled so long
That they are a race of children . . . and their plans
Are a child's plans, playing with sticks and mud. We
    have never
Gone back, our people . . . we never will! We'll push
These scavengers north, these eaters of dirt . . . we'll
    thrust them
North to the Lakes, take the St. Lawrence from them,
And leave them the eastern seaboard only so long
As they can hold it! That is what we drink to!
Who drinks with me?
[*The men are motionless for a moment, then come for-*
ward to fill the glasses.]
There is a play that we perform at New Year's . . .
In which the men of Taos, retaliating
Against the Comanches, don Comanche war-paint,
Trail feathers in their hair, and charge like Indians,
And return victorious. And there's a final scene
That shows a silent field, with fallen men.
I was a young man then but I fought in that battle,
And others who fought there are still here. It's grown
To be a legend . . . but it was more than legend.
Out to the east a hundred miles there lies
A ring of bones still whitening in the wind

Where you can count them. Seven hundred men
And not one left alive. The Comanche nation
Never struck back. It was never a nation again.
Tomorrow the Americanos camp at Cordova.
They won't get farther. And before they wake we sur-
    round them,
This time with rifles, and a hundred years from now
Our children's children, passing through that valley,
Will count the white-picked skeletons and remember
Who turned the Americans. If any pause,
Thinking this is not without risk, some will die, why
    true,
But it's death if we wait for them here! We struck them
    first,
And we'll not be forgiven! If any man say in his heart:
I have too much to lose, I dare not die,
Let him remember this is my wedding night,
I go from a bride's arms to battle. No man risks more.
Who drinks with me?

[*Each man lifts his glass. Suddenly they give a thunder-
ous cry:* "Montoya! Pablo Montoya!" *They raise the
glasses to their lips.*]

CURTAIN

ACT TWO

ACT TWO

Scene: *The same room a little later the same evening. The men have eaten and drunk and the remains of the food are on the table. A stack of long-barrelled rifles has been placed at the outer door, and the guests are beginning to file out toward them.*

A Few Women, *among them* Raquel, *come in to clear away.* Diana *is not in the room.* Martinez *is seated, waiting.*

Montoya

Let each man take his rifle as he goes. I take mine now. [*He does so.*] Sleep as long as you like tonight, as long as you can tomorrow. At sundown we start for Cordova, and it would be well to be fresh when we arrive. We should have drunk deeper if it were not for that, for the laws of the church run backward for me this evening, and I am to be married at midnight. All those of noble blood will return at that hour for the wedding. Goodnight to the rest.

The Men

[*As they go out*] Goodnight, Don Pablo.

97

MONTOYA

Goodnight, and sleep sound.

[*He turns toward an inner door and the assembly is dispersing quietly. A woman's voice is heard calling outside.*]

THE VOICE

Don Pablo! Don Pablo! Let me come in!

[MONTOYA *pauses and the others listen.*]

Don Pablo!

MONTOYA

Let her in.

THE VOICE

In the name of God, justice! He's killed my daughter!

[*A* MIDDLE-AGED WOMAN *enters, the men standing aside. She is followed by a* SOLDIER *who leads* MATEO, *a Spaniard, the latter wearing a bandage round his head.* NUNA *comes in after them.*]

THE WOMAN

Don Pablo . . . will you hear me?

MONTOYA

What is it, Valeria?

VALERIA

My daughter's murdered!

MONTOYA

By whom?

VALERIA

Carlotta's murdered! Mateo killed her!

MONTOYA

Mateo?

MATEO

Why, yes. I killed her.

MONTOYA

Why?

MATEO

For no reason.

MONTOYA

Answer me.

MATEO

Why does a man kill a woman? Let the others answer!

VALERIA

He had no reason! He came home and greeted us . . .
and then he went to her room and strangled her!

MONTOYA

Mateo?

MATEO

That is so.

MONTOYA

You're ready to die for it?

MATEO

I have no defence. Do what you like with me.

MONTOYA

Who knows what lies behind it? Come . . . there are
women here. What was the cause?
[*There is no answer.*]
Maria?

MARIA

Don Pablo . . . she was Mateo's wife.

MONTOYA

Mateo won't touch you. What gossip have you heard?

MARIA

Don Pablo . . . [*She pauses.*]

MONTOYA

Yes?

MARIA

At the time of the massacre one gringo escaped. It was
supposed he carried news to the north.

MONTOYA

We know that.

MARIA

It is said Carlotta warned him.

MONTOYA

Nothing more? There should be more than that.

MARIA

Nothing more was certain.

CRISTINA

[*Under her breath*] It was certain enough.

MONTOYA

Cristina?

CRISTINA

She brought all this on us. And she deserved it.

NUNA

They lied about her . . . lied!

MONTOYA

Be quiet, Nunita! How? What have you known?

CRISTINA

I've heard her talk.

MONTOYA

What did she say?

CRISTINA

She came to the market one day not long since, when
Mateo had beaten her . . . and said she'd have her
satisfaction.

MONTOYA

Well?

CRISTINA

She said that she had borne bastards to Mateo in the
past and would bear him bastards again. She said that
the men of the north thought all women angels and
treated them so, but the Spaniards believed all women
devils and therefore made devils of them . . .

NUNA

[*Whispering*] Lies, lies!

MONTOYA

That was all?

CRISTINA

No. We taxed her with knowing too well how the northerners treated a woman . . . and she said we would all
bed with northerners before the year was out, and be
glad of the change.

MONTOYA

Who else heard this?

CRISTINA

Raquel.

MONTOYA

Raquel?

RAQUEL

It was what she said. I heard it.

MONTOYA

Nunita . . . she was your mother. What judgment shall
I lay upon Mateo?

NUNA

They lied about her, always!

MONTOYA

And shall Mateo be punished? I make you judge of this.
What you say shall be carried out. Does he live or die?

NUNA

You make me the judge?

MONTOYA

Yes.

NUNA

Then kill him! . . . No, no . . . it was true . . . Oh,
God, now I know it was true about her! Let him go! . . .
Let me go now!

MONTOYA

Yes, go, Nunita.

[NUNA *goes out.*]

And you, Mateo, take your rifle from the stand. You are
no less one of us than before. If my wife had done as
yours or spoken as yours did, I'd use the same measures.
Let those women beware whose eyes have wandered.
Wait! What was the name of the man who escaped
through Carlotta?

CRISTINA

They called him Captain Molyneaux.

MONTOYA

We were betrayed then. And through Carlotta. Mateo,
there was more reason than you knew for what you've
done. It was Carlotta's doing that we were surprised at
the pass. The blood of every man killed was on her head.
We were beaten by treachery, not by the north! By God,
it's true!

HERMANO

It is true! And you were right!

MIGUEL

You knew this all the while.

MONTOYA

We've put our finger on the traitor, Miguel! And we

know there was a traitor . . . and by that same token
we know the next time we meet them will be another
story.

HERMANO

She may have had an accomplice.

MONTOYA

There's no doubt of it. And we must find him, too. That's
what I want to do now.

HERMANO

We'll leave you, then.

MONTOYA

But I'll see you? [*He gives his hands to* MIGUEL *and*
HERMANO.]

HERMANO

Yes.

MONTOYA

And you, Don Miguel . . . and Don Fernando?

DON FERANDO

Within the hour?

MONTOYA

Near midnight.

DON MIGUEL

Expect us, Don Pablo.

[*The ricos go out, leaving* MONTOYA, MARTINEZ, AN-
DROS, FELIPE, FEDERICO, MARIA *and* RAQUEL. MONTOYA
*sits, seeming weary. The women continue clearing the
table.*]

FELIPE

Pablo, you ate nothing. I watched you. Be mortal for a
few minutes, now . . . and touch some meat and wine.
[*He offers a plate.*]

MONTOYA

No, no. Let the others eat. I think more clearly without
it. Wait . . . lest it should be said that I have refused
you anything . . . [*He takes a morsel of meat with his
fingers and washes it down with a gulp of wine.*] No
more.

FELIPE

Come now. I was famished. You're still hungry.

MONTOYA

Not when I'm about to fight, Felipe. Have the sons of
Montoya never felt it . . . a fever in the liver so devour-
ing that food is impure? No, no . . . you're young.
There's an ancient belief that wisdom comes with age,
and the twenties are the time of passion. It's for that
reason they choose old men as judges . . . men who
will have outworn the lusts of flesh and blood and be will-

ing to rule impartially over the sins of youth. But all this
is a fallacy. For wisdom and justice we must depend on
the young; for madness in devotion to a cause, for all
madness, you must go among their elders.

FEDERICO

You say this to reprove us.

MONTOYA

Tonight let us have no reproof among the Montoyas.
No. I said it in excuse for you both, Federico. When a
man is first a man a little fire is kindled in him for his
race and his cause. If he is a man worthy the name he
blows this fire to a flame . . . and it burns up in him to a
conflagration. It burns in me now so white-hot and steady
that I look at my hand in wonder seeing that it doesn't
tremble . . . there's such a roaring of living fire inside,
such a war of seething heat that sweeps my brain and
nerves. It's a thought for your state should you ever
govern, Felipe. Make no old men judges.

ANDROS

General Montoya . . .

MONTOYA

Wait. Make the old men soldiers. Old men are swift,
violent, crafty, lecherous, unscrupulous in winning, re-
lentless in defeat, putting their cause before their af-

fections. Young men are much too tender, much too true.
When I was lost on the hills tonight, and some thought
me dead, I was hidden in a cave with three companions,
because the rifles of the trappers had swept the trail.
And I heard a voice calling my name. Up and down the
pass it went, calling my name. It was your voice, my
son, and you were risking your life needlessly. Had I
tried to reach you I should have been killed, and I lay
there, nursing my wrath at the enemy, knowing when
next we met them our rifles would outnumber theirs. Had
I been young as you I would have tried to warn you and
been slain for my trouble. And I learned then that in a
battle youth is too tender and too true. You should
have known that if I were dead it would do me no harm
to lie a night in the snow, that if I were alive I would find
my way alone.

FELIPE

And if you were wounded?

MONTOYA

Then better one wounded than two. But if you dream
I might hold this against you, my Felipe, you are wrong.
You are a kind and loving son. Only, when you are older,
as old as Federico, you will not take these chances. Federico is already wiser. He came home, and he was here
before you.

FEDERICO

I'm not good at riddles. Am I to gather that I've displeased you, sir?

MONTOYA

I am never displeased by superior wisdom. With what could I be dissatisfied, Federico? [*He lays a hand each on his sons' shoulders.*] These are tall brothers, in every way worthy. Go, and make yourselves ready for the wedding. Lie down if you are weary. It will not be for an hour yet. Tomorrow, too, you can rest . . . we won't start till evening. And whatever happens, this has been true . . . that I have been proud of you both, and have trusted you. That I have looked forward to an old age which you would lighten, one on either side.

[*He turns.* FELIPE *and* FEDERICO *start to go.* RAQUEL *suddenly throws herself at* FELIPE's *feet.* JOSEFA *enters and stands near the door.*]

FELIPE

What is it? Who is this?

RAQUEL

Ask him for me, in God's mercy. Ask him.

FELIPE

Who are you? [*He raises her face with his hand.*] It's Raquel. What shall I ask him?

RAQUEL

Only ask him, and let him say.

FELIPE

About Pedros?

RAQUEL

[*In agony*] Yes.
[FELIPE *turns to* MONTOYA.]

MONTOYA

Pedros? You've had no news?

RAQUEL

Nothing.

MONTOYA

Federico, he was your officer.

FEDERICO

He hasn't returned. I know nothing further about him.

RAQUEL

Pablo Montoya, you know. I can take your word.
[FEDERICO *goes out.* JOSEFA *looks at him. He avoids her eyes.*]

Montoya

I should say that Pedros would be alive. Yes . . . if I know Pedros.

Raquel

Then he is. [*She rises*] Thank you, senor. [*She goes out, and the other servants follow her.*]

Montoya

Andros?
[Felipe *goes.*]

Andros

You wanted me?

Montoya

Bring me the three prisoners.

Andros

Yes, Don Pablo.
[*He goes.* Josefa *comes forward.*]

Josefa

If I can be of use, Pablo, only let me know what you would like to have and it will be done. There may be preparations no one else could make so well as I.
[*He is silent.*]
I am no longer angry, Pablo. You will do as you will
. . . and I shall consider it just. Even this wedding

. . . I will help with it if I can. It is your house. The
women in it are yours. . . . If I rebelled at first, you
must forgive that. It has not been easy, but I accept it
now.

MONTOYA

There will be no preparations. One thing you can do.
Tell Diana that I wish to see her.

JOSEFA

Yes, Pablo. [*She goes out.*]

MONTOYA

What devil has poured his unction on that bitch?
She wish me well? There's something in this house . . .
I knew it when I came in . . . there's some snake's pur-
pose
Under this crawling. Federico, too.
He looked at me smiling, but there was that in his eyes
That wished someone dead and damned. Have you talked
to him . . .
Or to her? What have they said?

MARTINEZ

Nothing that's secret.

MONTOYA

Meaning you won't tell me. Because you think
It's better I shouldn't know. But, by God, I will.

MARTINEZ

You imagine this!

MONTOYA

Friend, I imagine nothing. I see and act.
I've seen two things that I'll find the bottom of
Before tomorrow. . . . I saw that I was betrayed
At the pass by someone within my ranks . . . and I saw
When I came home . . . that it was only my coming
That balked another betrayal!

MARTINEZ

As to the pass,
I know nothing of it . . . if we were betrayed
God help you find the traitor . . . but for the
   other . . .

MONTOYA

The other I'm sure of. If Federico glanced
About him like Felipe, and took my hand
With the same pressure . . . but no, his conscience eats
Into his brain . . . and he crawls, and Josefa
   crawls . . .
Felipe's done nothing he regrets. His eyes
Look back at you clear as a lake. And I think I know
What's bitten Federico. He's looked too long
At Diana, and wants her. And that explains Josefa.
I've watched her with Federico. She's willing that I
Should marry Diana and cut Federico off

From hope of her. And now I have one son.
One son only.

MARTINEZ

Pablo, when a man grown gray
Loves a young girl, he peoples the wind with rivals.
But even if this were true of Federico,
Isn't it natural enough? If she should love him
Could she be blamed? I could swear it isn't true,
But if it were . . .

MONTOYA

He's a man, I believe! Son or not,
My path has never been crossed! I'd cut him down
Like cactus!

MARTINEZ

Pablo, youth turns to youth
Inevitably as water seeks a level.

MONTOYA

And a son to a father's wife when she's young?

MARTINEZ

She's not
Your wife yet!

MONTOYA

She will be.

MARTINEZ

At our age men may have lust, but the day of love
Is over with us. A woman as young as Diana
Wants more than desire.

MONTOYA

Why, then, you know more than I do,
About women's needs, my priest. So far as I've known
What they want's desire, and when they get it they're
    happy,
And also they're in love. I've heard these lectures
From churchmen on the subject of lust. But I know
And you know, too, there's nothing a man's more proud
    of
Than his lust for a woman, and nothing a woman prizes
More highly in a man. Since before the beginning
Of knowledge women have given where gifts were re-
    quired.
A woman goes to the stronger, as land and nations
Go to the stronger. There's not one title to land
Or possession in any empire that isn't based
On a thousand murders . . . not one life in a nation
That wasn't nursed in a thousand conquered women!

MARTINEZ

You are the people's idol, Pablo. They look
On you to free them, and keep them free. This marriage

Detracts from you a little. It's something to smile at
When they meet to gossip.

MONTOYA

Let them laugh if they like.
They won't laugh in my face! The drivelling bas-
        tards . . .
You saw how they climbed on their asses and made for
    the hills
When they thought I was done for! No village of half-
    wits will set
My laws for me! I take the woman I choose,
And God can't help him who gets in my way!

MARTINEZ

God won't help him
Who gets in the way of what's coming.

MONTOYA

Of what that's coming?

MARTINEZ

The times are changing. Mexico's a republic.
The English to the north broke from their kings. We're
    here
Like a little island of empire, and on all sides
The people have a share in what happens.

MONTOYA

And that's what you've meant
By your printing press . . . and your teaching the
  peons to read!
Do you want a republic here?

MARTINEZ

I want to save
What we have, Pablo. They're not all peons. They look
To the north and south, my friend, and take stock of
  themselves,
A little, and wonder why one class of men,
Or one man out of that class, has it all his own way
In the province of Taos.

MONTOYA

If so, it's because you've taught them
To think they can think.

MARTINEZ

Not so. It came without asking,
Like an infection. There's only one cure for it,
And that's to seem to offer them from within
What's offered them outside. Give them books and
  schools,
And the franchise if they want it.

MONTOYA

You're my friend, José,
And have been, but this difference between us
Is deep as hell, and as wide. You fight the north
Because you want to keep your place. In your heart
You want what the north wants! But I fight the north
Because I despise what it stands for! Why should they
    think
About government, these peons? They're happier
With someone thinking for them! Why should the young
Take rank above their elders?

MARTINEZ

We must give them the shadow
Or they'll want the substance.

MONTOYA

Begin to make concessions
And they turn to a mob and tear you to pieces! Show
    them
You're afraid of them, and they're wolves! But let them
    see
That you're the better man and they're sheep, and your
    dogs
Can herd them without fences! . . . And shall women
    choose men?
Are they so much wiser? All your reforms fall in

With this plague from the north that enfeebles us! God's
　name,
I think you mean well! You've been my friend, but what
You teach is poison to me!

MARTINEZ

An enlightened people
Could be ruled more simply . . .

MONTOYA

All rule is based on fear . . .
On fear and love . . . but when they know too much
They neither fear you nor love you! Teach them too
　much
And you tear your empire down, and what you have left
Is what there was before there were empires! This
Is all your progress . . . and they won't thank you
　for it.
Nor will the women. They don't want freedom! But
　they'll take it,
And laugh at you for giving it!
[*The* TRAPPER *and* TWO OTHER PRISONERS *are brought
in guarded.*]

MARTINEZ

Then the marriage goes forward?

MONTOYA

Must we have this again?

[MARTINEZ *bows and goes out.*]
[*To the* 1ST TRAPPER.]
What is your name?

1ST TRAPPER

Senor, I have no intention
Of telling you my name nor anything else.
If you insist on one I'll give you the wrong one.

MONTOYA

Good, you have spirit. You're the leader then.
That's what I wanted to know. Your name, sir.

2ND TRAPPER

James.

MONTOYA

What kind of name is that?

2ND TRAPPER

If you want my full name
It's Humphrey James.

MONTOYA

Were you at the pass tonight?

2ND TRAPPER

Yes. I was there.

MONTOYA

Have you searched them?

ANDROS

We took their arms.
That's all there was.

MONTOYA

Let me see them.
[*An armful of weapons is brought forward.*]
And who are you?

3RD TRAPPER

I'm a prospector. I wasn't with the others.

MONTOYA

So this one's a coward.
[*He turns to the weapons.*]
Whose dagger is this?

ANDROS

[*Pointing to the* 3RD TRAPPER]
It was his.

MONTOYA

And now I know you're a liar.
I know this dagger. Where did you get it?

3RD TRAPPER

I bought it . . .
In Santa Fe.

MONTOYA

[*To himself*]
This dagger belonged to Pedros . . .
And I heard Pedros' voice after the battle.
He was alive then. There could hardly be two like this.
It's impossible. This one's a coward and liar.
And Pedros is dead. Search them again. Take off
That hunting shirt.
[*To the* 1ST TRAPPER.]

1ST TRAPPER

I think not.

MONTOYA

Take it off him!
[*The guards peel the shirt from the* 1ST TRAPPER.]
Toss it here.
[*They toss it to his feet. He touches it with his foot.*]
Put it on. Must I bring it to you?
[*The* 1ST TRAPPER *takes up his shirt.*]
Search the next.
[*They search the* 3RD TRAPPER.]
Take that shirt off him.
[*The shirt is tossed to him. He examines it with his foot.*]
Look through it. There's a paper in it.

[ANDROS *rips the shirt with a knife and takes out a map,
which he hands to* MONTOYA.]
By God, I was right!
They've been in my house. They were leaving here when
   we met them.
Where did you get this?

3RD TRAPPER

I didn't know it was there!

MONTOYA

[*Taking up the man's dagger*]
Where did this come from? This is Pedros' dagger.
Do you want to die the way he did?

3RD TRAPPER

He gave it to me.

MONTOYA

Who?

3RD TRAPPER

[*Indicating* 1ST TRAPPER]
He did.

MONTOYA

What's his name?

3RD TRAPPER

Captain Molyneaux.

MONTOYA

What else did he give you?

3RD TRAPPER

Nothing.

MONTOYA

Did he tell you
Why you were to carry this? Quick . . . speak.

3RD TRAPPER

No, senor.

MONTOYA

Were you in this house?

3RD TRAPPER

No.

MONTOYA

Tell me, senor Captain,
Who gave you this map?
[*The* OFFICER *smiles without reply.*]
You are all three to die,
You know . . . unless there is one of you who is willing
To tell more about this.

OFFICER

We'll die anyway, boys,
So keep your mouths shut.

MONTOYA

Even to an enemy
I keep my word.

[*To the* 3RD TRAPPER.]
Do you want to live or not?

3RD TRAPPER

The Captain was in the house. He brought two
    papers . . .
And gave one to me to carry, and one to him . . .
And we went separate ways.

MONTOYA

Search this man again.

2ND TRAPPER

Search me all you like. There was a paper,
But you won't find it. I burned it.
[ANDROS *searches the* 2ND TRAPPER.]

ANDROS

There's nothing on him.
It's true he burned something.

MONTOYA

When?

ANDROS

Outside in the jail.

MONTOYA

You sons of fools!

ANDROS

He threw it on the fire.

MONTOYA

What was in that paper?

3RD TRAPPER

Senor, I don't know. . . .

MONTOYA

But you have an idea. . . .
Come, we shall get along, we two. I promise you,
You'll live, and I don't lie.

3RD TRAPPER

They were talking about
A settlement . . . the captain was going to arrange
Not to destroy the town . . . because he owned it.

MONTOYA

Not to destroy Taos?

3RD TRAPPER

Yes, senor, because
This house was his.

MONTOYA

And who had signed that paper?

3RD TRAPPER

Senor, I don't know . . . and that's the truth.

MONTOYA

[*To the* OFFICER]
Someone had signed away this house to you,
And in return you were to pacify
The officials at Santa Fe.

OFFICER

The lad's a fool,
Don Pablo. He'll tell you anything you ask for,
He's making this up to save his hide.

MONTOYA

With whom
Did you make this agreement?

OFFICER

If you want a story from me
I can tell one fast enough. I negotiated
With a priest called Martinez.

MONTOYA

That is a lie. . . .
Go on. If you tell enough lies I'll know the truth.

OFFICER

Senor Montoya, I know the fix I'm in
As well as you can tell me. You're a hard man,
But I never met a Spaniard harder than I am. . . .
And you won't frighten me. The worst you can do
Is kill me or torture me. Well, the Indians tried that,
And they know the game, but I kept my mouth shut.
  You
Can say or do what you will, I give no one away. . . .
And I tell nothing. But if you have the time
I'd like to speak a word about this business,
Quite without malice.

MONTOYA

Good. You wish to advise me.
Proceed. Advise.

OFFICER

You've killed the governor
And a number of our citizens. Now, by what right
The government at Washington first laid hold
Of New Mexico I don't know. So far as I see
This land belonged to you Spaniards, but you were
  adrift
From Mexico . . . and you're not protected by
  Spain. . . .
There's nobody helping you but yourselves. Whatever
Your rights may be you'll lose. The government sent

A force to put you down, and it had to go back.
It wasn't sufficient. Well, they'll send another . . .
And if necessary another . . . they'll send an army
If they find they have to . . . and the more you resist
The worse it'll be. Taos will be destroyed,
With every man, woman and child, if you hold out,
And there's no point in it. It's a fertile valley,
And a handsome town, and it's rich. If you were willing
To lay down your arms, and concede some part of the place
To American ownership, you could keep the rest
And the war would be over . . . and a lot of lives saved, too.
If it goes on it's plain murder.

MONTOYA

[*To* 3RD TRAPPER]
One more question.
Where did you get this dagger?

3RD TRAPPER

He let me have it.
[*Indicating the* OFFICER.]

MONTOYA

You took it off a corpse?

3RD TRAPPER

Yes.

MONTOYA

Then who killed him?

3RD TRAPPER

Killed himself.

MONTOYA

More lies?

3RD TRAPPER

No, no, it's true . . . he killed himself!

MONTOYA

Pedros killed himself?

3RD TRAPPER

I don't know his name . . .
He brought a message to the captain before the bat-
  tle . . .
And afterward, after the battle, he came again,
And pretended he had a message, only this time
He tried to kill the captain. He had no message
This time. It was a ruse. They took him out
To shoot him, but he was too quick for them.

MONTOYA

What did he say?
Remember what he said.

3RD TRAPPER

When?

MONTOYA

Any time . . .
Whatever he said.

3RD TRAPPER

I wasn't near enough
The first time he was there, but afterward,
After the battle, when he'd drawn his knife on the cap-
tain
And we were taking him out, he said he'd thought
He was bringing a message to mislead us, but then
He found he'd betrayed his own people, so he came
back
To kill Captain Molyneaux. He called that back
To the captain when we were taking him away,
And then he killed himself.

MONTOYA

Pedros was true then . . .
Captain Molyneaux, will you tell me the name
Of the man who betrayed me?

OFFICER

No.

MONTOYA

You can have your life,
I have no interest in taking it.

OFFICER

No.

MONTOYA

And whether
You tell me or not I'll find it out.

OFFICER

I say no!
And no's my answer!

MONTOYA

This is strange behavior
For a man about to die. Are there other gringos
As stubborn as you?

CAPTAIN

Well, get it over with!
If you think I'm stubborn you've got a lot to learn!
You're used to peons and Indians!

MONTOYA

You prize your stiff neck
More than your life, it seems! You're proud of that,
And in your country it may be that the dogs
Are better than their masters . . . but not here!
Here you bend your neck or you don't live long.
Goodnight to you.
[*He goes to* ANDROS *and they speak a few words.*]

3RD TRAPPER

Senor! Your promise! Senor!

MONTOYA

You may live,
But it's no compliment. Send in Narciso,
I saw him outside.
[*The prisoners are led out.* NARCISO *enters.*]
Narciso, Raquel has asked me
For word of Pedros. Was Pedros lost?

NARCISO

I don't know,
Don Pablo.

MONTOYA

But he's not here.

NARCISO

No.

MONTOYA

And I'm quite certain
I heard his voice after the battle. He was, I think,
Federico's officer?

NARCISO

Yes.

MONTOYA

You've taken his place?

NARCISO

Yes.

MONTOYA

When were you appointed?

NARCISO

An hour ago,
Or a little more.

MONTOYA

Narciso, I'm sorry to say this,
But there's something strange about Pedros' disappearance,
And it reflects on you.

NARCISO

Pablo, I'm also sorry.

MONTOYA

And that's all?

NARCISO

Why . . . no. Pablo, perhaps I know
Where Pedros is, but it's something I'd keep from saying
As long as I could.

MONTOYA

Where is he?

NARCISO

I think he crossed
The line to the Americans.

MONTOYA

Why do you think so?

NARCISO

He quarrelled with Federico after the battle
And set off across country alone.
[*There is a long pause.*]

MONTOYA

With Federico. And what was said
In this quarrel with Federico?

NARCISO

I don't know that.
I didn't hear it . . . but they were very angry
And almost came to blows. I heard the noise.

MONTOYA

You heard not one word from this quarrel?

NARCISO

Let me remember . . .

No . . . not a word. I couldn't make out at the time
What they were incensed about.
[DIANA *comes to the door. She has changed her dress.*]

MONTOYA

Come in, Diana.
That will do, Narciso. Your name is cleared.
But send Federico to me. Tell him I wish
To lay our plans for Cordova.
[NARCISO *goes out.* MONTOYA *takes up the map and
puts it in its place. The dagger he puts in his belt. He
brings out a casket and sets it on the table.*]
This is a holiday dress. You are ready?

DIANA

Yes.

MONTOYA

It becomes you. I wish a man might look
Behind a woman's eyes, Diana, and see
What lies there. You veil your eyes from me.

DIANA

Now?
[*She looks at him.*]

MONTOYA

Even now.

DIANA

I'm sorry.

MONTOYA

No, don't be sorry, but this is a world
No man can trust much, even at best . . . and when
He gives his name to a woman, he must know as near
As he can how much he can trust her. Those closest
    to us
Have most to betray. I've been betrayed tonight . . .
Virtue's gone out of me, and out of this house.
Let me see your eyes again. Diana?

DIANA

Yes?

MONTOYA

What can you say?

DIANA

I don't know.

MONTOYA

Are you afraid?

DIANA

Yes.

MONTOYA

Afraid of Pablo Montoya?

DIANA

Yes.

MONTOYA

Is it because I'm older than you . . . and have power?

DIANA

Yes.

MONTOYA

Yes, perhaps. Let me see your eyes again.
I think that's what it is. . . . This dress becomes you.
Whatever you wear looks its best on you, Diana.
That's why I want you to wear a few jewels tonight
That haven't been worn since this house was built.
They are waiting
For someone to wear them who'd be worthy of them.
[*He takes out a tiara.*]
Take down your hair.
[*She loosens her hair.*]
This is to be your own . . .
And it's a dowry to be proud of.
[*He fastens it on her.*]
No matter
What the future may bring for me or you . . .
Keep it for your fortune.

DIANA

I do thank you.

MONTOYA

Thank me better. Have you no better thanks?

DIANA

Yes.

MONTOYA

Take my hands. Kiss me.
[*She does so.*]
If I have sensed
What happiness lay in you . . . I was wrong . . .
    you are richer,
Sweeter than I could know. Let me look at you . . .
I want to see what bride it is I take
Before the others are here. This is your hair.
This is your hand. You stand thus. Now
Could you kiss me, and kiss me as a lover kisses?

DIANA

Yes. Must it be tonight?

MONTOYA

You are a gentle girl, Diana. Perhaps
One takes advantage of that, and assumes that you
Will understand what's strange, forgive what's left out
In the way of courtesy.

DIANA

It's not that.

MONTOYA

For the rest,
You have known a long while what was destined for
    you.
You came here a captive child, with other captives,

And played at my feet as a child, and, watching you,
And weary of tongues and unfaith, and women who
    seem
To love where they hate, I lost myself in dreaming
Of a child-wife, who would love where she seemed to
    love
And give herself purely. You grew in beauty, too . . .
Grew maiden-like, flower-like, woman-like, and still
    kept
Your candid eyes that never lied, and I knew
If you were mine, you'd be wholly mine. I could rest
In that. You come of an alien race, somewhere
From the north . . . I've lost trace of where, but a
    woman's mind
And heart are in her eyes . . . and you could be
    trusted.
And so I told you of this, and you were troubled
As a maiden is . . . but I wanted the world to know
Where I had chosen, and wanted to prepare you
Softly as might be. If I come suddenly now
To fulfill my promise, it's not as I would have had it,
But we run risk of death tomorrow, and I
Should not be willing to die before I'd tasted
For once, this one happiness. Am I forgiven
Now, for my abruptness?

DIANA

I've made myself ready.

MONTOYA

There are two kinds of happiness, to win
In battle, because that makes you one with those
Who are your people, and to share a love
With one who loves you . . . because then, for an in-
    stant
A man is not alone. But when one shares
Himself and all he has and then discovers
Too late, that he was mocked, and the woman mocked
    him,
There's no such loneliness on earth. I've loved
And given, but without return. Always I've known
Too late that I was alone.

DIANA

Could that have been . . .
Don Pablo, because you demanded . . . instead of
    asking . . .
Because you took as your right, whatever you wanted,
Instead of wooing for it?

MONTOYA

But not with you!
With you I have been gentle . . . Only give me all
Your faith, and you shall have mine! Will you give me
    that?

DIANA

I have no wish to rule . . . !
I don't care for that! Let me live where I can,
Humbly, anywhere . . . and marry humbly
And be forgotten! You have many things
In your life! I could be forgotten!

MONTOYA

You said you would give me
What you could.

DIANA

Yes.

MONTOYA

I won't ask more than that.
You are a child still, and I seem grim to you
And you're afraid. But as for running from me
And hiding from the world, and marrying humbly . . .
That you don't mean.

DIANA

Oh, yes.

MONTOYA

There was never a woman
Worthy to be a woman, who wouldn't choose
A man she could honor rather than a handsome face
Growing on a peon. Yes, a woman will take
One-tenth of a man she can honor, and share him with
    others

Rather than breed with his servants. You, too, will
    know that
When you are older . . . and love me, and be proud.

DIANA

I thought I could bear it. But I can't! Pablo Mon-
    toya,
Have pity! You are great! You won't need me. Oh, for
    God's love,
Have pity on me!

MONTOYA

Child, I love you. If you
Had ever been in love you would know there was one
    thing
A love cannot do. It cannot let go.

DIANA

But I could.
If I were in love I could take all my life in my hands
And give it to him I loved, and turn away
And never see him if he asked it!

MONTOYA

Yes,
But you are a woman. And something in what you say
Teaches me you are more of a woman than you could
    be
If your heart were empty. Who do you love?

DIANA

No one!

MONTOYA

You love my son! I had evidence of this before
But I wouldn't believe it. When Josefa came to me
Smiling, to hurry the wedding, I knew it then.
She wishes you married to me. What has there been
Between you and Federico?

DIANA

Federico!
Nothing.

MONTOYA

No . . .
But there would have been had I not interrupted it
By returning awkwardly. You've been untrue
Already to me at heart. You're like the others,
A woman, inconstant, deserving of no better
Than the others, and giving no better. But know this
    about him . . .
If there were no other reason that he should die
He'd die for this, but there are other reasons.
He's sold us out here, or tried to, and he fought
Against us at the pass, like the whelp he is,
And my nest shall be cleaned of him! I loved him
    well . . .
Stood ready to share my name and fortune with him,

And he sneaks like a jackal in his father's house,
Stealing his wife and his place, surrendering
To thieves that he might share! Go, and be ready . . .
But guard yourself . . . for I know you now . . .
Look not
To right or left from me. For I swear to you
That if the son I love were to lift his hand
Toward yours, he'd die . . . and as for Federico . . .
Count him dead. Go! Why should you look on my tor-
  ment?

[DIANA *goes out. The village is heard singing far-off
the same song with which they welcomed* MONTOYA
back. He sits listening. FEDERICO *comes to the door.*]

FEDERICO

Their spirits have come back. You hear them?

MONTOYA

Yes. They'll follow tomorrow, and gladly too,
If we can keep them singing.

FEDERICO

They sing enough.
Too much sometimes.

MONTOYA

Is there something on your heart,
Federico?

FEDERICO

No. I think not.

MONTOYA

You start queerly
Sometimes, as if the opening of a door
Might bring ill-fortune. As if something lurked
In corners here.

FEDERICO

It may be I'm not so easy
When things are happening, as I will be later
When I've seen more.

MONTOYA

Are you clear enough in your mind
To lead one section of the attack tomorrow
Without failing me?

FEDERICO

I think so. What are the plans?

MONTOYA

If we can time ourselves to reach Cordova
Just before dawn, before the horses wake
To graze, we'll find the troops camped in the valley
Along the stream. They'll have to take the trail
That brings them there . . . and they'll stop there,
   for the water

Is hard to reach further on. If we attack
From one side or the other, they'll have the trail
Before them, and they'll escape, or most of them . . .
But if we make a division of our forces . . .
Attack with half the rifles on this side
And meanwhile plant an ambush on the other
Where they'll run into it unprepared, we'll have them
As neatly bottled as could be wished. Now I
Can't be on both sides of the camp. If you
Will lead one-half our men around Cordova
And wait where the gulch is narrow, our campaign's
    planned
And we can sleep tonight.

FEDERICO

That's excellent.
It's almost certain victory.

MONTOYA

More than that,
It may be that not one will get away.
That's what I want . . . to take them by surprise,
And leave not one alive.

FEDERICO

That's possible,
But not too likely . . . they can climb like goats . . .
These hunters. Some would escape.

Montoya

Which would you choose . . .
To make the first attack at this side, or lead
The detachment round for the ambush?

Federico

Let me have
The post of danger. I'll go on ahead
And wait for them where it's narrow.

Montoya

And you're sure
You can hold them there?

Federico

Trust me.

Montoya

Your officer . . .
Narciso, is it?

Federico

Yes.

Montoya

I could wish it were Pedros.
We lost our best man in Pedros.

Federico

He was hardy.

Montoya

And faithful, too. One could trust him always.

I wonder at his being killed. I could have sworn
I heard his voice after the battle, among your men
As plainly as yours now.

FEDERICO

You heard his voice?

MONTOYA

It must have been an illusion. Such things do hap-
pen . . .
Voices come back from the dead . . . to testify
Or complain, perhaps, if their owners died unhappy.
And this is strange . . . I took this dagger from
A trapper prisoner. Was that Pedros' dagger?

FEDERICO

I think it was. From a trapper?

MONTOYA

Yes.

FEDERICO

That's like them . . .
To rifle the bodies.

MONTOYA

Well . . . Narciso will do . . .
But don't depend on him too much.

FEDERICO

I'll see
To every order myself. And let me thank you
For laying this trust on me.

MONTOYA

I think you'll be worthy
Of the trust I give you. Federico,
It's been borne in on me of late that I've taken
Too much to myself, and allowed no scope for the play
Of younger minds and hands. The estate is large
And I've kept too much to myself in its super-
    vision . . .
I can't do everything well. If I should give you
Half share in the ranch, would you stay here with me
    and keep it
As jealously as I have?

FEDERICO

I would indeed.
[*A marriage song begins outside.*]
But this . . . you don't mean this?

MONTOYA

Why, indeed I do.
I do mean it. And lest we let it go
And you think it out of mind, let us get the map
And make our choices.

FEDERICO

Let it go till later.

MONTOYA

No, bring it . . . bring the map.

FEDERICO

I can't accept it
Till you've had time to think.
I've thought a whole life-time!
[*A pause.*]

FEDERICO

After we meet them tomorrow.
[*He turns.*]

MONTOYA

Very well.
We'll let it go till later.
[FEDERICO *starts to go.*]
No, wait,
Good God, let's settle this little matter! We'll have
The map!
[*He goes to chest and brings it out.*]
Four thousand acres this side of the river,
And fourteen thousand in the flat, beyond. It's enough
To make a Yankee covetous, I admit.
[*Federico, terrified, is rooted where he stands.*]
But is that reason enough to cause a Montoya,
An elder son, trusted, acknowledged heir,

To draw a line down the center, and auction off
His father and his brother, and a whole village
To keep his skin from danger?
[MARTINEZ, FELIPE, DIANA *and* JOSEFA *come in.*]

MARTINEZ

This is the time you set,
Is it not, Pablo?
[*The marriage song comes nearer.*]

MONTOYA

Why yes, it is time. Come in . . .
Come in, Felipe! Come in all of you
And watch his face while I read him a history
Of what he's done! Look at him!
[The NOBLES *of the village, four or five in number,
enter with their wives. They are ushered in by* NUNA,
who goes out at once.]

FEDERICO

What do you mean?
What have I done?

MONTOYA

Be patient. I'll tell you. This map
Has a line drawn across it . . . a line dividing
Your share from the man you sold out to . . . you
    were to get

Immunity to live here for that share!
Look at this dagger, too! Look hard at it
And let nothing show in your face when you remember
Whose dagger it was, and how much a better man
Pedros was than you are! Pedros is dead.
He killed himself when he knew what you were about
And what he'd helped you with. It was Pedros who car-
    ried
The word to the other side to avoid the pass
And strike us on the flank. And the man who sent him
Was Federico.

FELIPE

It was true then?

FEDERICO

Someone has lied
To you about this.·
[*There is a volley outside, then two more in quick suc-
cession.*]

MONTOYA

Someone told me the truth,
And that's his reward for it. The Yankee trader
Who traded with you is dead. Look, look, Felipe . . .
That was my eldest . . . that one there with the face
That twitches . . . but the deed is cancelled now.
The party of the second part is dead,
And the party of the first part's dying.
[ANDROS *and* NARCISO *enter.*]

FEDERICO

But it was annulled when you came back! And think . . .
You hadn't returned . . . it was supposed you were
   lost,
And I knew no other way to save our lives
And the lives in the village . . . was it treasonous
To take command when I thought I must?

MONTOYA

Look, Felipe . . .
Whatever love or promises I gave him . . .
Whatever was his as my eldest son, is yours,
Stand at my shoulder now . . . let me believe
One can trust a son . . . this is not easy, to send
A son to death. I'll try to forget that he's lived
And remember only Felipe. Why, look, he's not
And never was a Montoya. . . . See, he crawls . . .
Crawls again!

FEDERICO

I think you're wrong!

MONTOYA

That's better . . .
Stand up and fight me, at least. If I must kill you
At least die like a man!

FELIPE

Perhaps he's not
So much to blame as you think.

MONTOYA

I know the story
From beginning to end. It was his plot that brought us
Defeat on the mountain. Even then he was in touch
With the northerners . . . and even then he was woo-
    ing
The woman I'd chosen to marry. Weren't there enough
    half-breeds
To help you populate the valley, that you
Must approach my woman, and win her over to you
And away from me?
[*To* DIANA.]
How proud of your choice are you now . . .
Now that you know him?

FEDERICO

I won Diana from you?

MONTOYA

Yes . . . that too.

FEDERICO

You fool! It was Felipe.
She loves Felipe now!

MONTOYA

Yes, tell your tales . . .
Lie out of it if you can.

JOSEFA

It's true, Don Pablo . . .
She loves Felipe!

MONTOYA

And you, too, have your reasons
For wanting me to think so!
[*To* ANDROS.]
Take out Federico
And chain him at the plaza gate, let him feel
What it's like to hang in irons before we hang him
The last time for the buzzards!
[ANDROS *and* NARCISO *start to lead* FEDERICO *out.*]

FELIPE

You won't do that!

MONTOYA

By God, I will!
He could hang a thousand years, and it wouldn't pay
  me
For what he's done!

FELIPE

But I say you won't!

MONTOYA

Why not?

FELIPE

He's your son . . . my brother . . . you can't stake
  him out
Like a bear to be tortured . . . !

MONTOYA

Only I will!

MARTINEZ

Don Pablo. . . !

MONTOYA

Get on with him! Get him out before this knife
Of Pedros' finds a home in him!

MARTINEZ

Don Pablo!
[*They take* FEDERICO *out.*]

MONTOYA

Damn you! One thing I could bear . . . that he'd betray me . . .
I'd swallow that . . . I'd have let him live . . . a
  coward . . .
But the other I won't take!

JOSEFA

Then why do you send
The wrong man out to be chained?

MONTOYA

You fiend . . . be quiet! . . . Felipe!
This is not true?
[*A pause.*]

FELIPE

It's true that I love Diana.
I can't deny that.

MONTOYA

And she loves you.
[FELIPE *is silent.*]
You do love him?

DIANA

No, no . . . I swear it . . .
There's been nothing, nothing . . .

MONTOYA

And you've been willing
To let Federico suffer . . .

DIANA

Oh, Pablo, believe me . . .
I'll be a true wife to you.
[*She goes to him.*]
I'll be true and faithful,
And do all you can ask.
[*She kneels.*]
Forgive me if I

Have been silent when I might have spoken, or seemed
To turn away when you came to me. It's true
I'm young, and you are older . . . and I've been
　frightened . . .
That I couldn't help . . . but I'll be kinder
And give you all you ask . . .

MONTOYA

Do you love Felipe?
[*She is silent. There is the beginning of a babble of
voices outside that increases in volume slowly.*]

MONTOYA

Speak! Do you love Felipe?

DIANA

But it's not his fault!
I loved him first, and he never spoke to me . . .
And there's been no crime . . . no touch . . .

JOSEFA

She lies . . . we found them together . . .
In each other's arms!

DIANA

Only when you were lost
And hadn't returned! Punish me, Pablo. Felipe
Is your son . . . and wouldn't dishonor you!

MONTOYA

I'm blessed
With dutiful sons, it seems. They think of me only . . .
And of my wife!
[*The voices outside are louder.*]

DIANA

Pablo . . .

MONTOYA

Be silent! You'll drive me
To something I must keep my hands from, plead-
    ing . . .
Are you so hot for him?

MARTINEZ

This is not more or less
Than you could hope for, Pablo. Since it comes now
Before this marriage, it won't come later on.
If you'd been married, every year that went by
Would have brought it nearer, inevitably. Somewhere,
Some time, she would have loved and been loved where
    her youth
Was certain to lead her . . .

MONTOYA

What are you mumbling?

MARTINEZ

I say
There's no crime in it except your own.

MONTOYA

You knew this!

MARTINEZ

It was certain to come.
[*There is a shout outside. It trails off into single
voices, indistinctly heard:* "What does he say?"
"They've sworn to destroy the village!" "Three hundred thousand men!" "He talked with the northerners." "Will you listen to him or his father?" "He's a
Montoya, as much as Don Pablo!" "I say, loose him!"
"Let him go!" "Damn you, come no nearer!" *There is
silence, then* FEDERICO *is heard as if a door had been
opened in the passage.*]

FEDERICO

[*Outside*]
You have seen a village
When it was in ruins . . . no life, the people living
Somewhere in the hills! . . . But this will be worse
    . . . they're in thousands,
These Americans . . . they'll come like locusts . . .
    flies . . .
They'll come when you least expect it . . . not one
    escapes . . .

And they could be placated . . . my father's
   mad . . .
Crazy . . . he wants to die . . . wants you all to
   die . . .
And you've been fools and followed him because
He gave you rifles! . . . Why, if he gave you war-
   paint
Like the Indians you'd do as well!
[*The crowd breaks into a louder babble.*]
[ANDROS *enters.*]

ANDROS

I'm sorry, Don Pablo,
But I think you should interfere before your soldiers
Listen to more of it. Federico's surrounded
By a great crowd at the gate . . . and when they
   asked him
How he came there, he told them that he had arranged
A peace with the north which you had repudiated . . .
Also that you intend to execute him
To keep this knowledge from them.

MONTOYA

Say that again.

ANDROS

Federico's spreading sedition at the gate.
They've all surrounded him because of his chains,
And he tells them they can never win against

The English of the north . . . many believe him . . .
Or at any rate, they're shaken.

MONTOYA

You will stay here
And wait for me . . . all save Andros.
[MONTOYA *and* ANDROS *go out. Soon afterward the
noise of the crowd is suddenly hushed.*]

DIANA

Felipe . . . you . . .
Go quickly . . . I won't see you . . . but I'll love
   you . . .
Go . . . the other door . . .

FELIPE

You must think lightly
Of me, Diana. Would I go, and leave you?

DIANA

Felipe . . .

FELIPE

Will you come with me?

DIANA

If we were caught
You would be killed . . .

FELIPE

But we wouldn't be caught . . .

DIANA

Yes . . . yes . . . there's only a moment, Felipe . . .
    you waste
Your whole life waiting. . . !

FELIPE

Come then . . .

DIANA

And bring your death on you?
You'll die if you stay here now . . . you'll die if I go
Along with you . . . but you alone could escape . . .
He'll let you go if I'm here . . . but if I were with you
He'd never forgive you, and he'd never give up
Till he'd hunted us down!

MARTINEZ

All this is true, Felipe . . .
Be off, and swiftly . . . and I'll tell him I advised it.

MONTOYA

[*Outside*]
Stand back from him! Stand back!

DIANA

Quick! Now, Felipe! Oh, God, will you wait for
   him . . .
Till he comes back? You must live. . . . If he should
   kill you
And I were to blame, how could I live?
[*There is a great shriek from the crowd . . . then
silence and one voice.*]

THE VOICE

Don Pablo!
Don Pablo! Your son!
[*There is complete silence, then the steps of* MONTOYA
*returning slowly in the corridor. He comes to the door
and enters, his head bowed, the dagger in his hand. As
he comes to the center a great splash of scarlet is seen
to have appeared on the front of his white hunting-
shirt.* NUNA *and* RAQUEL *appear silently in the doorway, a few* OTHERS *behind them.* RAQUEL'S *face is a
tragic mask.* MONTOYA *stands with bowed head for a
moment, then tosses the dagger to the center of the
table, where it sticks trembling, and turns his eyes
toward* FELIPE.]

CURTAIN

ACT THREE

ACT THREE

SCENE: *The same. The act opens some minutes after the close of Act II.*

FELIPE *and* DIANA *are guarded and about to be led out.* MONTOYA *stands near the table, breathing as though he had come through a scene of violent altercation.* MARTINEZ *faces him, evidently his antagonist. The* RICOS *have drawn nearer. The rear door is open and* MANY PEOPLE *have collected silently to listen, unnoticed by the* RICOS.

MONTOYA

[*To* MARTINEZ]
I say he dies!
[*There is a slight gasp and motion among the people.* MONTOYA *notices them.*]
Andros, clear out those slaves!

ANDROS

Out that way, Narciso. Take them with you.
[*The crowd murmurs.*]

SANTOS

What's he done?

GRASO

He's done nothing.

DIEGO

[*Loudly*]

Pablo, what's the charge against Felipe? We want to
know.

ANDROS

Are you going?

[*The crowd is put out and the door closed. Only*
RAQUEL *and* CRISTINA, *who were making preparations for the marriage, remain behind.*]

MONTOYA

[*Quietly, to* MARTINEZ]

I say he dies.

[*To* FELIPE.]

A woman hated me once

And tried to poison me. It happens it was your mother,
Yours and Federico's. She had loved me at first
And borne me two sons, but she grew to hate me then
As fiercely as she'd loved. I knew this. She tried
To hide it with soft words, but one night at supper
She turned her back for a moment, pouring my wine,
And then set a glass for me, and one for herself.
I looked in her eyes, and changed the goblets, and
drank,
And she took the challenge and drank . . . she was no
coward . . .

And died before my eyes. I have this poison
Of hers. It's quick and painless, and stops the heart.
I found it, and still keep it. There's enough left
To end her generation! You were all three traitors,
All three in different ways. It's fitting to end it
With her own potion. And go on alone.
Take them out.
[DIANA *and* FELIPE *are led out.* MONTOYA *faces* MAR-
TINEZ.]
In the future, Father Martinez,
Remember that your business is with the church.
Your authority stops there!

MARTINEZ

What you do tonight
Concerns not you alone, but all Taos. I plead
For our city . . . not for the church, not for my-
　　self . . .
And I say call back Felipe!

MONTOYA

Have I lived so long
That I hear a priest give me orders?

MARTINEZ

Things are not as they were!
From now on you'll listen to more than yourself!

MONTOYA

You heard
What was charged against Federico, heard his reply!
I heard it . . . and rather than any other hand
Should be lifted against him, I killed him. He was my
    son.
His life was mine. It's not what a man would
    choose . . .
To strike down his own son . . .

MARTINEZ

No man has challenged
The death of Federico! But to kill Felipe
Endangers us all!

MONTOYA

He also is my son,
And his life's mine!

MARTINEZ

Then the north does win!

MONTOYA

It wins if he lives!

MARTINEZ

Whether he's guilty or not
To kill him means we're beaten. You'd never gather
Your army round you tomorrow. There'd be no army;
Your leadership depends on the trust they have

In your strength and wisdom. If you execute Felipe
They'll no longer respect you. The news will spread
That Pablo Montoya's raving in his house
And murdering his sons. Can you command them
With that in their minds?

MONTOYA

Is this happening to me . . . to Pablo Montoya,
To hear this mouthing! Not since I was a man
Has my rule in this house been questioned . . . nor in
    this city!
Am I likely to accept it now?

MARTINEZ

I remind you only
To think of Taos first . . .

MONTOYA

The north wins in Felipe
If he has his way! When sons turn against their
    fathers
And get their will by it, all our rule goes down
And order with it. Our state's built on that . . . but
    no more . . .
Not if Felipe can defy me, and keep
What he got by defiance! You fool, the north itself
Attacks us from within, and if it conquers

In Taos, what will it matter if Taos is taken
And conquered from the outside?

MARTINEZ

Don Miguel . . . Hermano . . .
You must see this!

MIGUEL

Martinez, in these days
An anarchy drifts down from the north upon us,
Even here where we guard ourselves, and some give
    credit
To new strange gods, and deny our ancient customs.
The rights of the old, the rights of fathers give way
To the rights of sons. Children look up with envy
At family possessions, and snatch when they can;
And some say, "Good. Let the old men look to them-
    selves."
And some say justice should be dealt by the rabble
On young and old, on rich and poor alike.
So thought Federico. You see where it led him.
You see where it leads us all.

HERMANO

I have a house
Of my own, and I have sons, and I'd rather they gave
No orders to me.

FERNANDO

Nor I.

MARTINEZ

There have been two things
I wanted . . . that we might save the house of Mon-
toya,
And that we should save Taos. Perhaps we can't have
both.
In that case it's best to save Taos. Pablo Montoya
Can sign his own death warrant, and yours, Don
Miguel,
And every rico's, but not mine, and not
The city's.

FERNANDO

You're one of us, Martinez, you
Will go as we all go!

MARTINEZ

No.

FERNANDO

From the very beginning
You sat in our councils.

MARTINEZ

We part over this!

MONTOYA

Let him go.

CRISTINA

[*Whispering*]
Now, Raquel.

RAQUEL

Don Pablo!

MONTOYA

[*Without looking at her*]
What is it?

RAQUEL

I'm only
A woman, Don Pablo . . . but I've lost a hus-
    band . . .
I've lost Pedros, and he was true to you
When others failed you. Remember that and forgive
    me . . .

MONTOYA

Forgive you what?

RAQUEL

For saying this: Felipe
Must not die, Don Pablo! Whatever he's done
He must not!
[MONTOYA *is silent, looking at* MARTINEZ.]

JOSEFA

You've been dismissed! Is once not enough?
[RAQUEL *and* CRISTINA *go out.*]

HERMANO

What do you mean to do? Where will you go?

MARTINEZ

I go with your peons outside . . . and ask what they
    ask!
They're right this time, and you're wrong . . . and
    they have the power
To say what you must do!

MONTOYA

Let him go!

MARTINEZ

I followed
Pablo Montoya, believing that through his strength
And leadership we dared take up the challenge
The north threw down. I believed there was a chance
Of making this province too costly for them. But when
Montoya tosses his leadership away
And tears his house down quarrelling with his son
It's time to think of my people.

MONTOYA

Your people?

MARTINEZ

Yes, mine!
They're no longer yours! You abandon them to keep
Your pride! We all know what hangs over us!

We're at war with a nation that outnumbers
Our little state by millions! This counter-stroke
You've planned might make them wary, hold them
    off . . .
Make them regret what they've started! But fail in
    that,
Lose the next battle, lose the people's confidence,
And your history's ended! Kill Felipe, and you do
    fail . . .
Keep him with you, and you may win!

Montoya

[*Coldly*]
Think more clearly, Martinez.
Suppose Felipe lived, and lived in my house.
She would be Felipe's or mine. Suppose she were mine,
And I knew she had loved Felipe. Is that a thing
A man can bear? Or suppose I gave her up,
As I might, and she were Felipe's, and lived with him
Here in my house. Is that a thing a man could
Bear, and live? Not I.

Martinez

The city of Taos
Will live on, then, and the church . . . and I my-
    self . . .
But this is the end of the ricos.

FERNANDO

You intend to betray us?

MARTINEZ

What could I betray? They know who leads here
And who's committed with him. I'm no friend to
The north, and I'll never be . . . but I can live with it
If I have to . . . and so can the peons! Go fight your
    battle,
And when you're broken, I'll gather what's left of our
    city
And we'll live here as we can! But, good God, what's a
    woman
To weigh one way or another when the question's only
How to save the house of Montoya, and saving that,
Save all of you?

HERMANO

And why should our winning or losing
Depend on Felipe? He's but one man among us
And a young soldier . . .

MARTINEZ

You haven't seen that yet?
That Montoya no longer governs Taos? . . . That
    you . . .
All of you . . . hold your places here only so long
As the peons think you worth fighting for? You heard

What Raquel said . . . Felipe must not die!
You thought nothing of it. She was only a woman . . .
Unworthy to give you counsel, but she spoke for all
    Taos . . .
And all Taos waits at your gate to hear the an-
    swer . . .

MONTOYA

They heard my answer!

MIGUEL

Pablo, there's truth in this.

MONTOYA

[*To* MARTINEZ]
I think you'd rather the ricos
Were gone, and the town was yours to rule as you
    pleased,
Federico-fashion!

MARTINEZ

Have you known me so long,
Pablo . . . and you can believe that?

HERMANO

It's true, if Felipe
Could live, Don Pablo . . .

MONTOYA

Am I alone among you?
Fernando?

FERNANDO

Speak to Felipe, Don Pablo. Too much
Depends on this.

MONTOYA

I am alone.

FERNANDO

It's true
They govern us now. If they find us unworthy to die
    for,
Why should they die for us? And they won't do it.

MIGUEL

No.
[MONTOYA *regards his guests silently, making up his
mind.*]

JOSEFA

How can you ask it of him? How can you dare
To ask this of Montoya?

MONTOYA

Be silent.

JOSEFA

I know
When to be silent. I've hated him in my time,

And also I've loved him . . . but there's not a man
 among you,
And not one outside, with half his strength or cour-
 age . . .
And yet you dare ask him to humble himself before
His people and his son!

MONTOYA

Every man asks
What he must to save himself. Well . . . I can give up
To Felipe . . . to save the city. I've lived enough
To face that much. I'd rather Felipe lived.
This is no longer my city, but Felipe's.
Arrange it as best you can. I leave this to you,
Hermano. Call him in.
[*He turns slowly and goes out.*]

HERMANO

[*To* ANDROS]
Bring Diana first.
[ANDROS *goes out and returns with* DIANA.]
You must not be frightened,
Diana. Stand here . . . and let me ask you only
Two or three questions. You're not to be punished,
 neither
You nor Felipe. It's not a thing forgiven
Easily, that you've forgotten a pledge
Sworn to Montoya, but there's nothing for us to do

But erase what's happened. Can you forget Felipe
Utterly, Diana?

DIANA

No.

HERMANO

But you
Will promise to be a true wife to Pablo Montoya
In word and deed?
[*There is no answer.*]
You must answer yes to that
Or we can't save him.

DIANA

Yes.

HERMANO

And whatever has passed between you and Felipe
Is cancelled and ended?

DIANA

Yes.

HERMANO

Why, see now, the world
Is yours again to live in. This is not so bad,
You'll find . . . to trade a first maiden inclination
For a whole world. Let us have Felipe, Andros.
[ANDROS *goes out.*]
You need not stand now, Diana. That's the last ques-
    tion,

And Felipe's to live.
[*She sits.*]

MARTINEZ

Are you so sure of that?
Montoya meant to give Diana up
To Felipe. He said as much. Do you mean by these
   questions
That Diana goes to Pablo?

HERMANO

I do mean that.
And why not? What we want is to save Felipe . . .
Does it matter how?

MARTINEZ

Diana will promise whatever
She must to help him . . . but he won't surrender
   her . . .
He'll choose to die . . .

HERMANO

I think not.

MARTINEZ

He'll choose to die . . .
And you'll be driven to threaten him. If he still
Refuses . . .

HERMANO

He won't refuse.

[FELIPE *is brought in.*]

Felipe, it's been decided
That we must go back to where we were . . . blot out
What was said here . . . and what led to it. If we do
   that
Our lives can go on as before . . . if not, this night
Will leave terrible scars on all of us. What we could do
To palliate your offense, we've done, and will do,
Not only for your sake, but for your father,
And the name you bear in this province. If you will
   promise
To put Diana out of your mind . . . why then
Nothing will be held against you. I'm delegated
To put this to the question. Answer wisely, and keep
Your place in our hearts and our city. You'll do this?

FELIPE

Yes, if I can.

HERMANO

Then first . . .

FERNANDO

Ask him first what there's been
Between him and Diana.

FELIPE

Senors, if my father
Questions me I'll answer whatever he asks.
Let him ask me himself.

HERMANO

He left this to us.

FELIPE

As to Diana . . . I knew she was my father's . . .
But I did love her . . . and do.

HERMANO

She loves you?

FELIPE

Yes.

HERMANO

But you're willing to relinquish her?

FELIPE

I am a prisoner,
Don Hermano. Why should I be asked
To relinquish Diana willingly, when you know
You can compel me to do whatever you like?
[MONTOYA *re-enters and waits in the rear.*]

FERNANDO

Because you must live! And your father and you must
   both live,

And live here in this house! She will be his wife!
Say something that will make us understand
That this sickly love is ended, before it ends
Our hopes in you!

FELIPE

How can a man promise that?

FERNANDO

He can promise whatever he has to!

FELIPE

I have no heart
To oppose my father. . . .

FERNANDO

Then why do you oppose him?
That's what you're doing. We ask only your promise!

FELIPE

[*Impatient*]
I give it!

MONTOYA

Never mind his promise . . . I ask
No promise from him, nor from her. I have this to say,
Which I should have said before. Let the north come
    down. . . .
And all the devils to fight on its side. . . . Let the
    peons

Yell at my gate till they're speechless. . . . Let all of
  you
Warn me as you have . . . this is still my place
And my house and my city! Let him promise or not
As he likes, he'll do what's required of him while he's
  here,
And Diana likewise! Let the north come down!
I'll be as I've always been . . . and live as I've
  lived. . . .
And fight as I've fought . . . ! Let Felipe live! You
  might
Have spared your promise. I meant to let you live,
Promise or not. . . .
[*He turns.*]

FELIPE

Pablo, let me speak to you!

MONTOYA

Why, speak.

FELIPE

I?

MONTOYA

Yes.

FELIPE

You've forgotten my name then, Pablo?

MONTOYA

What do you want to say?

FELIPE

Why have we grown
So far apart? When I looked for you on the moun-
    tain . . .
I loved Diana then. . . .

MONTOYA

You looked for me hoping
You'd never find me.

FELIPE

Pablo . . .

MONTOYA

Are you afraid?
Another Federico?

FELIPE

We were always friends,
Pablo . . . even tonight . . . tonight in this room,
And though I seem to blame for what's come between
    us,
I can't help trying to tell you . . . that I'm
    sorry. . . .
And I wish we could be as we were. . . .

MONTOYA

He is a coward.

FELIPE

And I'm no coward!
I tell you that when I sought you on the mountain
I sought you because I loved you! I sought you as you
Might have looked for me if I'd been lost! If I'd found
    you
Dying there in the snow I'd have given my life
To save you! Yet I knew then that I loved Diana. . . .
And more than I loved you . . . and that if you lived
You'd keep her from me! . . . It was you who were
    wronged
By my loving her . . . not I . . . but I never chose
    it!
Never in my life have I wanted to hurt you
Or thwart your wishes! Only, now, since we're caught
In this thing together, and neither can help it, why
Are you suddenly a stranger?

MONTOYA

Because I know
What happens when two men meet face to face
And want the same woman! Brothers they may be,
Or father and son, but they hate each other! You
Both hate and defy me.

FELIPE

Pablo, does what I say
Sound like defiance?

MONTOYA

I have no more desire than you
For a feud between us. I loved you as you loved me.
I want to love you now. But there's no tie
Between two men that holds when both of them love
A woman, and one has her. This will happen to us. . . .
Be sure of it. It happens now in your eyes.
You wished me dead in the snow. You tried not to
   wish it,
But you wished me dead.

FELIPE

It's true. I tried not to wish it,
But I did wish you dead.

HERMANO

He's given his word,
Don Pablo, and he'll keep it. Give him your hand.
He's a better son than you think. Let it go at that.

MONTOYA

[*Turning away*]
Yes. Let it go.

Felipe

And I'd rather not give my hand,
And rather it didn't end this way. My father
Has an instinct in such matters.

Miguel

What do you mean?

Felipe

I'm a son of Taos. I've been loyal to Taos,
And its ways are deep in my blood, but still it's true
That I'm a rebel at heart. Somewhere within me
Something cries out: Let us go! Let us be free
To choose our own lives! Sometime, if you let me live,
It will be the worse for Taos that I'm alive. . . .

Hermano

Damn you, be still!

Felipe

No . . . I tell you my father
Makes no mistakes in such matters! I'd be a traitor
To my house and my cause if I lived. I tell you that
To save you from it!

Miguel

Do you want to talk yourself
Into dying quickly?

FELIPE

It may be a better death
Than I'd have later, better than I think's likely
To come your way, Don Miguel . . . or any of you!
I don't know when it will come . . . you'll have vic-
    tories,
Perhaps, for a while, but before they're through with
    you
The armies of the north will crush you in
And drive a last few of you to this crag to die
And keep you here till it's ended! Till it's all ended,
The last of Taos, the last of Spanish power
North of Mexico city!

FERNANDO

And you're for the north,
That's what you mean?

FELIPE

How could I be for the north
When all my people, all my friends, and my life
Are rooted in Taos? I've fought on your side and
    mine,
And I'd do it again . . . but still I'm not so blind
But what I can see that if the laws of the north
Were to judge between us, my father would be in the
    wrong,

And I'd be held right! And it would be just! But here
A girl goes where she's sent by her father, and when
She's chosen by an old man who can pay for her
Or who has her at his mercy, she's his, and a slave,
And all the women are slaves here! (That's why you
  can't trust them!)
And the men are slaves! Yes, I am myself no better
Than a peon, nor any of you! I've earned the right
To say this. I'll die for it!

[DIANA *rises*. MONTOYA *turns on* FELIPE.]

MONTOYA

When a woman once bears a bastard
She'll bear more than one, count on it! Federico's
  mother
Was also yours, and all three hated me,
And all three tried to betray me! You think I don't
  dare
To send you after them . . . you think we'll pick
Some justification for you, and cover it over
Because you're only half guilty. If you were a man
Worth saving you'd be one thing or the other. This
Is too cowardly to be treason! Half-coward, half-
  traitor,
More snake-like, more deadly, more to be despised
Than Federico himself. You've chosen sides
Against a man who can take a handful and make it

An army by what he dares! They'll come to me . . .
Come fawning to me, they'll crowd under my banner
And fight against their own, these northerners,
When they know the man I am! You should have known it,
And you've failed as a man and my son! Hermano!

HERMANO

Felipe!
Do you want to drag us all down?

FELIPE

Let him free Diana
To make her choice! And remember that Federico
Was right about the north!
[*A silence.*]

HERMANO

Are we in accord in this?
[MIGUEL *and* FERNANDO *assent silently.* HERMANO *turns to* MONTOYA.]

MONTOYA

Leave them to me.
[*The stage empties of all save* MONTOYA, FELIPE *and* DIANA.]
Why, yes, Diana may choose.
Do you choose Felipe . . . or me?

DIANA

To go with Felipe.

MONTOYA

You know what it means?

DIANA

Yes.

FELIPE

There's no question of that.

MONTOYA

She'll choose for herself.

FELIPE

Diana!

DIANA

Would you have me live . . .
And live on after you, a slave? They say
I'm a northerner by birth! A woman of the north
Chooses the man she'll follow! I have my own right
To choose to die!

MONTOYA

And since you choose Felipe . . .
I was a traitor to myself to want you
With your northern blood and face. It's just as well.
[*He sets out a carafe and glasses.*]
It's fitting to end it

With her own potion . . . and go on alone.

[*He pours two glasses and takes out a little phial.*]

Drink quickly! Let me see the last of her spawn

Put under ground!

Take with you my own treachery to myself. . . .

This woman that stands here . . . and let me go out
alone

To face my world again!

[*He lifts the phial, but instead of pouring it in the
glasses, holds it in his hand.*]

Wait, wait, I'd forgotten!

[*He sits.*]

There's something I'd forgotten. It was a dream.

Is this a dream that we were standing here

And I had sentenced Felipe? I've dreamed it before.

There's something unreal about it. Don't drink, I said,

It may be poisoned!

[*He starts up.*]

Do you know what's true?

I'm old and alone, and my people fall away,

And the race is old and nerveless. The village is eaten

With doubt of me and my purpose. They're all de-
cayed

Under the skin. They bloom like health, but they're
rotten

And dying out. Why should they fight the north?

They'd rather surrender, and live here under Martinez. . . .

And so would Felipe. I killed Federico, but that
Was a last effort, desperate. No strength.
Till now I thought I was young. I've always been
    young,
The first man in the field . . . in any assembly
First there too. To youth and strength belong
The whole of the earth, and I've believed them mine
Because I was strongest. The eagle lives long, but at
    last
He grows old, his sight is dimmed, he misses
His stroke, and goes hungry on his crag. This thing
Comes to them all, eagle and kite alike,
And now it comes to me. I had a dream
That Spain was old, and her arts and ways were worn
To mockery, threadbare . . . her power was taken
    away. . . .
Her kings were impotent on her throne, her people
Impotent at home. The barbarians
Lifted new standards . . . that which once was right
Was right no longer, but wrong. The children's words
Were taken for truth . . . the old men stood aside
And listened to this new wisdom. A new race came
And said, There is a God over you who sets
A term to all things, to man and nation alike,
And your term is up. Felipe came to me
And said, love is not bartered in the new lands. . . .
Give me back my love. But this was no dream,
Or else my dreams are true. Our race is done.

The Spanish blood runs thin. Spain has gone down,
And Taos, a little island of things that were,
Sinks among things that are. The north will win.
Taos is dead. You told me this before,
But I wouldn't believe it. I believe it now.
Yes, and it's right. It's right
Because what wins is right. It won't win forever.
The kings will come back, and they'll be right again
When they win again. Not now. The gods are weary
Of men who give orders, playing at God. And why
Should a man, an old man, looking forward to nothing,
Take pride in breaking men to his will? Meanwhile
The years creeping up at his feet, and all he has
Going down around him? And then to stand there,
    alone,
Helpless . . . an old man, playing at God. Go out,
Leave me, be together, be free! In all Taos
There's only one man who could not surrender and
    live,
And his heritage is darkness. I drink to your mother.
She had her way.
[*He drinks from the phial.*]

FELIPE

Pablo!

MONTOYA

And you have yours.

FELIPE

Never! Pablo, believe me! Hermano, Miguel.
[*He goes to the door.*]

MONTOYA

Stay here . . . I need no crowd around me to die!
What do you want to do?

FELIPE

To bring help. . . .
[MARTINEZ *enters.*]

MONTOYA

It's useless . . .
If that's what you mean. I'd rather you were here,
Felipe. Forgive me. It begins to blind me already.
[*He reaches for a chair and sits.*]

FELIPE

If I could help you . . .

DIANA

Or I.
[*She kneels beside his chair.*]

CURTAIN